"*Changing Course* is a very important guide to the third age. The authors' innovative work has combined vital new concepts with practical help for those who are navigating the turbulent waters of change during this potentially thrilling time of life."
—PETER BRILL, M.D., Founder, The Third Age Foundation

"For many people *Changing Course* will redefine life after fifty. It describes the many positive choices we can all look forward to and how these choices should guide pre- and post-retirement behavior."
—WILLIAM C. BYHAM, Ph.D., Chairman & CEO, Development Dimensions International, Inc., and author of 70: *The New 50: Retirement Management: Retaining the Energy and Expertise of Experienced Employees*

"*Changing Course* is a valuable resource for boomers transitioning from well-defined productive years to unstructured retirement years. This book is about creatively designing your life in the "middle years," where fifty is the new forty or younger. This reality, along with the dramatic expansion of life expectancy, presents challenges for society and individuals for whom there are no role models. *Changing Course* is a necessary and valuable contribution to meeting these challenges. It is well written, the research is solid, and the language is clear—an easy, flowing read. The lessons are conveyed by personal success stories of how different people of vastly varied backgrounds and experiences applied six principles in creating a "successful third age." *Changing Course* is an indispensable aid in making one's life 'A Story Worth Telling.'"
—BILL SHIRLEY, Executive Coach and Consultant.

Changing Course

"*Changing Course* is the right book at the right time.
As millions of Boomers are plotting the next acts of their lives,
it is indeed fortunate that this invaluable guide
comes along just when we need it."
—JAMES O'TOOLE, author of *Creating the Good Life* and *Leading Change*

"Grab this book if you are thinking about the second half of life.
You will be richly rewarded with heartwarming stories and
practical advice from two seasoned wise men."
—JOHN R. O'NEIL, President, Center for Leadership Renewal,
and author of *Paradox of Success*

"*Changing Course* combines practical and theoretical wisdom
with inspiring, illustrative stories of third-agers who are making
the most of their post-midlife "bonus" years. The authors
supply valuable concrete suggestions for third-age
life planning to help readers follow suit. Committed readers
will not only discover many gems but also find themselves
on the path to a more vital, fulfilling third age."
—MARGARET L. NEWHOUSE, Ph.D., Founding President, The Life
Planning Network, and co-author of *Life Planning for the Third Age*

"As Boomers move into uncharted territory, many find themselves
face to face with the question: What next? These pioneers are
crossing into the frontier of an entirely new stage of life opening
up between midlife and old age, "The Third Age." These travelers
have few role models, and the available pathways are poorly
marked. Yet in the face of this challenging landscape they now
have a book, *Changing Course*, which can help them find new
fulfillment to accompany the great gift of longevity. Filled with
insight, beautifully written, and anchored in careful research, the
authors have written a book that is useful both for individuals and
as a roadmap for making the most of our aging society."
—MARC FREEDMAN, Founder, Civic Ventures, and author of *Encore:
Finding Work that Matters in the Second Half of Life*

CHANGING COURSE

Navigating Life after Fifty

WILLIAM A. SADLER, PH.D.
JAMES H. KREFFT, PH.D.

THE CENTER FOR THIRD AGE LEADERSHIP PRESS
CENTENNIAL, COLORADO
WWW.THIRDAGECENTER.COM

Published by The Center for Third Age Leadership Press, an
imprint of The Center for Third Age Leadership, LLC

Visit the *Changing Course* website at
www.ChangingCourseBook.com

Printed in the United States of America

Library of Congress Control Number: 2007924469

ISBN-13: 978-0-9793510-5-1
ISBN-10: 0-9793510-5-7

Publishers Cataloging-in-Publication Data

Sadler, William Alan.
    Changing course : navigating life after fifty /
William A. Sadler, James H. Krefft. -- 1st ed.
    p. cm.
    Includes bibliographical references and index.
    LCCN 2007924469
    ISBN-13: 978-0-9793510-5-1
    ISBN-10: 0-9793510-5-7
    1. Middle age. 2. Middle-aged persons. 3. Self-actualization
(Psychology) in middle age. I. Krefft, James H. II. Title.
HQ1059.4.S23 2007   305.244
                                           QBI07-600092

FIRST EDITION
First printing 2007

ABOUT THE AUTHORS

WILLIAM A. SADLER, PH.D., has been a professor, administrator, author, consultant, community leader, and speaker. Since receiving his doctorate from Harvard, Bill has authored five books. His last, *The Third Age: Six Principles of Growth and Renewal After Forty*, led to the formation of The Center for Third Age Leadership. Translated into several languages, in 2006 it was featured as book of the week by the Korean Broadcast System. For nearly twenty years Bill has been professor of sociology and business at Holy Names University, where he still teaches MBA leadership courses. He and his wife Sallie reside half the year in Oakland, CA and the other half in Maine.

JAMES H. KREFFT, PH.D., is president of The Center for Third Age Leadership. He works as a writer, consultant, and executive coach. In his second age Jim plied careers as a university instructor, Army officer, technical editor, Human Resources executive, and management consultant. He charged into his third age at forty-two when he left a major corporation. In addition to coauthoring *Changing Course*, he has written or collaborated on two other books and a screenplay since turning fifty-five. Jim has a bachelor's in philosophy and a master's and doctorate in English literature. He and his wife Lynn and their two children Michelle and Jim live in Colorado.

With gratitude to Sallie, whose love, companionship, intelligence, and sense of humor provide joy, challenge, and inspiration for sustaining growth.

—WILLIAM A. SADLER

To my wife Lynn, and to our children, Michelle and Jim, for teaching me what it means to be a husband and a father, and for having had the faith to journey with me even when my destination has seemed so far away.

—JAMES H. KREFFT

CONTENTS

PART TWO: POSSIBILITIES AND LESSONS

ACKNOWLEDGMENTS

WE ARE INDEBTED TO THE PIONEERING THIRD AGERS who generously shared with us their life stories of changing course. Colleagues at The Center for Third Age Leadership (CTAL) graciously read the manuscript, suggested ideas, and helped keep *Changing Course* on track: Nancy Cosgriff, Melita DeBellis, Bill Idol, and Mark Olken. We owe Ronn Williamson special thanks for also being part of our publication team. Other CTAL colleagues contributed by offering advice and insights: Melanie Abbott, Lora Abernathy, Gil Blount, Jan Byth, Barkley Calkins, Cindi Crutchfield, Tom Dudzinski, Jim Herring, John Lloyd, Tim Melson, Mike Mulcahy, Les Rosenbloom, and Jimmy Smith. Professor Gilbert Leclerc gave expert counsel on the new view of aging. We are also grateful to our designers: Aimee Carlos for the cover and Dianne Nelson for the book. Above all we most especially owe gratitude to our wives, Sallie and Lynn, for listening, reading, rereading, and making forthright suggestions all along the way.

INTRODUCTION

Sunset and evening star,
And one clear call for me!
And may there be no moaning of the bar,
When I put out to sea.

—TENNYSON, "Crossing the Bar"

GROWING OLDER OFTEN FEELS like skating on thin ice. For most of us living has generally been on firm ground. Much of the time we were pretty sure of what we had to do: go to school, get a job, make friends, stay healthy, support ourselves, and perhaps raise a family. Our charter was by and large clear and immediate, often compelling. Moving into the second half of life can be unsettling. This new terrain prompts perplexing questions. How far can I go? In which direction? What might I expect? What risks am I prepared to take? What's safe? What's dangerous? Do I have enough insurance? Enough money? Am I really ready for this?

We have yet to meet anyone racing ahead. How about you? Are you dying to be older? Most of us are proceeding tentatively, sometimes reluctantly. Some wish they could reverse direction, but that fantasy is delusional. Yet there is a good chance that what's ahead is considerably better than anything you've imagined. What does better look like? How can you achieve it? That's what this book is about.

Research into adult development and aging indicates that the landscape for the second half of our lives has been changing dramatically and positively. Your expectations, fears, and questions about the next period in your life are most likely based on past experiences and assumptions out of touch with new developments in the life course. As you skate along, chances are that what's ahead can be much different than your fears and prejudices might suggest. Your next journey holds more promise than you have prepared for. Does it really? How do we know?

Recent international studies have reported about not only increased life expectancy but also positive alternatives in aging. In this context our research for over twenty years has been tracking people who have been creatively redesigning their lives after fifty and exhibiting new, personal growth just when many people might—as conditioned by negative stereotypes of aging—expect decline. These creative people tell us, "This is the best time in my life." What they have been doing after fifty represents a possibility that previous generations for the most part simply did not have. We are talking about a first-time-in-human-history opportunity.

Perhaps the most pivotal discovery in our research has been that after fifty you and we have creative potential that enables us to direct and shape our lives to experience more meaning, enjoyment, purpose, vitality, and fulfillment than we could have expected as we crossed the bar into maturity. Outdated, debilitating aging stereotypes still proliferate in our culture and need to be replaced with reliable guidelines. In this book we show you how pioneers on the frontier of new possibilities have been creatively changing course, enabling them to transform the process of growing older in a radically different, highly positive way. Middle age is moving up from forty to our fifties and sixties.

The people in our research are showing us that now *older is much younger than we thought*. We all can learn from them. We shall provide you with perspectives and practical illustrations that you can apply to your own distinctive version of the second half of life, aging, and retirement, or whatever you choose to call it.

This book extends the research of Bill Sadler's last book, based on a twelve-year longitudinal study of several dozen people who redesigned their third age, a new middle period in the life course. Although a small sample, these people represent a broad mix of women and men. Their stories in *The Third Age: Six Principles of Growth and Renewal After Forty* showed alternatives to conventional patterns of middle age and aging. Do you think people are genetically programmed to begin degenerating in the fifth or sixth decade? Is a midlife crisis inevitable? Are human beings over the hill after turning fifty?

That's not what we have found. Individuals can initiate a process of growth that leads in a positive direction, postponing and transforming aging. The people in the last book and in *Changing Course* have been experiencing a *second growth* through the third age. How have they managed to do this? By carefully examining their development, Bill discovered six principles of second growth. His book shows how these principles can operate to initiate growth in all of us.

Readers from around the world have reported how that book has helped them recast a life scenario, clarify options to usual aging, get in touch with creative potential, experience renewal, and take practical steps for self-realization in the third age. We now have a new framework for thinking about the next stages in the life course; and the stories illustrate how the six principles of growth and renewal can be applied.

A year after *The Third Age* appeared, a dozen business professionals formed an enterprise to apply the growth principles to the workforce. Through consulting, coaching, workshops, seminars, and retreats, The Center for Third Age Leadership aims to help individuals and organizations design a productive and fulfilling third age. These programs based on the six principles have proven to be particularly appropriate for managing the transition from second age to third age, and for third age planning. Jim Krefft, a former executive and business consultant, and President of The Center for Third Age Leadership, joined Bill to continue learning from people who exemplify the option of creative growth in maturity. Our collaboration generated the additional research underlying this new book.

Based on our ongoing research, we believe that as people grow older they should want more, not less from life. Don't you? Don't we all want not just normal development but *optimal development* through the second half of life? That's our assumption. How can we achieve it? In the research that underlies this book, we've been asking: How can a person navigate life after fifty to expand her or his boundaries and keep growing? And how can second growth influence the way an individual designs and experiences retirement?

You should know that assumptions that most of us had ten or twenty years ago are no longer appropriate. Those ideas are now more likely than not just plain wrong. People today have options, resources, and experiences that previous generations did not have. In growing up, most of us have learned outdated lessons about growing older. It's time for us to unlearn those lessons and develop a different perspective.

When you look at your life as you grow older, where do you put the emphasis? On *growing*, or on *older*?

Instead of the latter, we have learned how you and we can creatively sustain growing for a fulfilling life after fifty. For most of us that emphasis on growing calls for redefining retirement, or whatever we choose to call it, as mindfully as we prepared for life and careers in the second age. The main purpose of *Changing Course* is to help you figure out how to do that preparation. We offer insights, principles, and practical guidelines to help you reflect on, dream about, and plan for charting a new course in your life. This book is different from the previous one in several ways.

First, most people whose stories fill this book are older than those cited in the previous one. *The Third Age* reported mostly on people growing impressively through their fifties. In *Changing Course* we have been asking people now in their sixties and seventies: how do you keep on growing? Some of these people were in the first book; others we have met more recently. Their stories show us how we can transform aging in the third quarter of our lives.

Second, the focus has shifted to making a successful transition into a new phase, often called retirement. The people in this book have been addressing the challenges of aging and retirement by *redefining both*. Most don't even think of themselves as retired. Many despise the term *retirement* and even refuse to use that label. Maybe you're like them, and dread taking retirement like getting a bad cold in winter. Our book offers options for finding your own cure for the common retirement.

The stories here are about people who have been able to free themselves of misconceptions and stereotypes and who have applied creative thinking about both their third age and retirement. This self-help book is also more practical than the last one, with both stories and lessons at the end of each chapter. We show how you, too, can tap your creative potential to change course for an adventuresome journey into your fifties, sixties, and seventies.

Third, the social landscape has been dramatically changing in the past ten years, affecting how we think about redesigning retirement and our lives. The new landscape offers all of us challenges, opportunities, and options never before available. In the twenty-first century we are in a new era that calls for radical rethinking about our life course, and revolutionary self-redirection. ·

Part One explores challenges and opportunities in the second half of life. First we look at retirement in its current setting and talk about why we need to redefine the concept. The second chapter shares what we have been learning from research about alternatives to usual patterns of aging. Understanding an alternative perspective can dramatically affect your experience of the third age, of retirement, and of life completion in the fourth age. In chapter 3 Bill updates his discovery of the six principles of second growth and shows how they apply to changing course.

With this new scenario, Part Two presents possibilities: stories of people who have inspired and instructed us in the experience of changing course. Chapter 6, in addition, also shows how individuals, professions, and organizations can benefit from our findings and apply them to *third age careers* that foster both personal and organizational development. In the final chapter Jim offers specific steps for third agers approaching retirement—how to get ready to change course—including five major tasks of *third age planning*. Each task serves as a countermeasure to one of five big risks for third agers approaching retirement.

We have filled this book with practical ideas for individuals, couples, families, and groups to shape a whole new way of navigating life after fifty. We hope that you use the book to stimulate your own fresh thinking about your third age and retirement, clarify your growth possibilities, and give yourself a new mental framework for planning the next phase in your life.

Our title is a metaphor for how you can adapt to *growing* as you get older. This is your voyage and your call. So get out your navigational charts and equipment—it's time to change course.

PART ONE

CHALLENGES
AND
OPPORTUNITIES

CHAPTER ONE

RETHINKING RETIREMENT

We are not permitted to choose the frame of our destiny,
but what we put into it is ours.

—HAMMARSKJÖLD, *Markings*

WHAT DOES **RETIREMENT** MEAN?

IN PLANNING THE NEXT PHASE IN OUR LIVES, whether we like it or not most of us need to come to terms with retirement. As our research got underway, we didn't like the word. After several years of investigation, we still don't like it. The people we have interviewed feel the same way. The word means "withdrawal," and implies idleness. "Retire?" said one man, who retired the first time fifteen years ago, "That's what you do when you go to bed at night. Then you go to sleep. That's not how I think of what I'm doing with my life now. I'm still waking up to new possibilities and reinventing myself." At sixty-five he sees the changes he has made since he passed fifty not as retiring but as turning points leading to new opportunities.

Retirement as we know it is a relatively new concept. It has been applied to the general population only recently, thanks largely to extended longevity, social security, and pension funds. Previous generations didn't live long enough or couldn't afford to retire. Most people had to keep working to survive. When the concept was institutionalized in the last century, the shelf life of retirement was only a few years, because average life expectancy was much shorter than today. If you could make it to sixty-five—and most people didn't—retirement gave you a period of leisurely withdrawal to enjoy the last days of your life without labor. This arrangement applied basically to men; women were mostly kept working in the home. If work was drudgery or physically debilitating, then retirement offered a desired respite, a well-earned reward of rest for years of labor. But in the twentieth century the nature of work for most people changed dramatically, and the idea of retirement has not kept up with these changes.

Unlike other rites of passage, like leaving home, graduating, getting married, or taking a job, retirement has been largely about endings, not beginnings. Retirement was the last stop and wasn't expected to last long. However, the unprecedented increase in life expectancy in the last hundred years makes this idea inappropriate. To retire has meant ending one's voyage to secure a mooring in a safe harbor. If redefined, however, retirement can challenge us to change course for new adventures. Most of us can count on living well past retirement age, however you define that point chronologically. We could spend more time in retirement than we did working. What are we to make of this phase of our lives that might last thirty or forty years?

For a start, we should take a hard look at what it has meant. In everyday usage retirement signifies *not-working*. The concept suggests a quiet life without productivity, challenge, and engagement. In their last book on the life cycle, Erik and Joan Erikson described retired people they interviewed as feeling unneeded, unproductive, and casting about for something meaningful to do. Retirement as it is practiced in our society, they wrote, "Seems to doom a large segment of our population to inertia and inactivation."

The film *About Schmidt* portrays an American businessman feeling isolated and useless after his company releases him into retirement. His life up until then had been totally focused on his job. Without it he feels lost. When he discovers his office has altered operational policies and thrown out his meticulous records of forty years, he feels betrayed. "What difference has my life meant?" he asks. "Very little," he concludes. Retirement stretches before him like a wasteland. Like Schmidt, many people experience the "retired" label as a demotion. One woman told us she stopped describing herself as retired: "People hear that and respond to me as though I'm in the same bin as last week's lettuce." "So how do you describe yourself?" "Well, I tell people I'm consulting. I'm not interested in doing that at all. It's just that consulting at least suggests that I'm still alive and *with it*."

Not all retirees experience a bleak existence. According to AARP many people are satisfied—but most do not report "ecstatic"—with retirement, in part because conditions have changed. People are not only living much longer, but many are also staying healthier and more active than previous generations. Also there are more financial resources available to them. In the last century most people who could afford to retire counted on small incomes from pension plans with defined benefits and social security payments. Increasingly, people have taken control of their pension plans with investments that allow flexibility. So they are freer to take what they need from investments they control to do what they want. Bumper stickers proclaim: "We're out spending our children's inheritance." Some people have used retirement as a form of self-indulgence. But certainly not most people.

Rather than seeing retirement as a period of idleness, more people are seeing it as a period of new opportunity. This prospect often includes freedom to spend more time with families, to invest in leisure activities and learning, to travel, and to find new work. Recent surveys indicate that 80 percent of Baby Boomers expect to work in retirement. Some people are already shifting from fulltime employment in one career to another career or to bridge jobs. Bridging gives them something to do and time to investigate possibilities for a new career. The people we've been studying are doing better than that; they have either started a third or fourth career or extended their professional lives in new ways. In chapter 6 we'll have more to say about developing third age careers as one alternative to usual retirement.

Although Boomers say they plan to keep on working, however, most companies have not yet opened up to take advantage of the resources older workers have to offer. Retirees may want work, but they don't easily find work that matters. People tell us that fulltime retirement is much less than they expected. It leaves them underutilized, feeling withdrawn from society and with too much time on their hands. They are unprepared for an abundance of unstructured freedom. Lee Iacocca's comment captures what many have experienced: "I flunked retirement." He failed because he did not invest in carefully planning for this new phase in his life.

Retirement is now lasting for decades, and it will increasingly be a stretch of time longer than the length of fulltime employment. Managing such a huge amount of time becomes a formidable challenge. So far many don't seem to be up to it. Like the Eriksons, we have heard retirees say that they feel marginalized and bored. It didn't surprise us to learn that elders now watch more television than any other age group. As one woman asked, "What do you do after eleven o'clock in the morning, after you've finished your chores, made your calls, and read the paper?" Retirement gives people a lot of time to ask questions for which they're not prepared.

HOW DOES RETIREMENT CHALLENGE US?

RETIREMENT NOW POSES some of the most challenging existential questions we have ever faced. One man, brave enough to voice them in a retreat for third age leadership, commented, "Now that I am retired I have time to pursue some big questions: Who am I and what kind of person do I want to become? Where do I want my life to go next? What legacy will I leave?" Like more people in this generation, he is also thinking about what work he wants to do next. He certainly does not see his retirement defined as not-working. "How can I find the work I really want to do in the next phase of my life?" he asked.

Individuals should address these vital questions in a planning stage long before entering retirement. But retirement planning programs and books don't typically explore them. Instead they focus primarily on financial planning, with attention to healthcare, new locations, travel plans, and leisure activities. Ironically, these resources generally take a busywork approach to planned idleness. They advocate new kinds of to-do lists to keep you from getting bored. As one retiree told us, "After six months I finished my first list and had to start another. My colleagues and I have nearly invented a new career of revising our to-do lists." Retirement planning too often takes a linear tunnel-vision second-age approach to the third age. In chapter 8 we shall be recommending third age planning as an alternative to what's usually offered.

We believe the whole concept of retirement needs drastic redefining if we are to prevent a massive waste of human potential. The redefinition of retirement has already started, as individuals become more mindful about their future and more invested in their own life after fifty. Virtually all the people we've interviewed, who might be considered to have retired, say that retirement does not apply to their unfolding lives. They are not idle, but engaged. They're advancing, not retiring. Helen Dennis, an expert in retirement planning, reports that we are experiencing a "retirement revolution." Conventional retirement no longer offers what people need. She has suggested dropping the term entirely and recommends that people focus instead on *life management* to achieve more meaning as they grow older. A sense of purpose, she believes, is what people are looking for.

So if we don't choose to use the label of retirement, what can we call it? Some people are inventive as they characterize this new phase in their lives. Some have called it *protirement*. A pair of career counselors has suggested *refirement*. A university scientist still working in his lab sees it as a *perpetual sabbatical*. One woman in our study tried retirement three times and failed it each time. "Retirement's the wrong word— what we need is renewal," she told us. In sharing his story, one former executive reported, "When I left the company after thirty years, I didn't retire. I graduated. And that means a commencement of something new and different."

We like the concept of graduation and will explore its implications in chapter 4. Although not using his term, the people in this study have been exploring new directions and changing course by creatively shaping their post-institutional lives. They are not making to-do lists; they are graduating, and sometimes graduating again and again.

More and more people have continued working in semi-retirement or have gone back to work, especially during the bursting of the dot-com bubble and the economic downturn that followed. Many people will probably combine working with retirement or use retirement to find new forms of working, if the economy opens up to older workers. Some people are already establishing the paradox of a *working retirement*. That idea is not an oxymoron; it's an emerging reality. In the near future retirement will not mean not-working. But there is presently a cultural lag between intentions and reality. Bridging is often the best people can come up with.

In spite of the professed desire of able, talented, mature people to continue working in significant capacities, companies do not seem interested as yet in retaining or hiring older workers. The workplace is still conditioned by false myths of aging. Many retirees suffer from enforced idleness or restricted opportunities, taking jobs beneath their capacities and experience. Volunteer opportunities are often worse, assigning richly talented people to mindless tasks: stuffing envelopes, handing out juice at a blood drive, or picking up trash along a highway.

Our society needs to change its outlook and policies to provide genuine opportunities for people of retirement age to make significant contributions in the workplace and the social sector. Our country has invested mightily in helping adolescents make the transition into the second age with multiple institutions—education, internships, youth programs, community and military service, and so on. At present we have no appropriate institutions to help people with the transition from second age to third age. We need to invent some. Otherwise we shall continue to squander much of our valuable talent.

In chapter 6 we'll show you how organizations and professions can redesign pre-retirement transition programs by using third age planning and third age careers. This innovative approach can harvest the wisdom of valuable, experienced leaders and employees and stave off an impending demographic crisis of an imminent shortage of competent professionals. We need social reconstruction to help redefine retirement as a possibility for a better society and a productive, truly fulfilling life. If not, we're going to squander billions of human years and trillions of days of opportunities. Do the math. A thirty-year life bonus multiplied by tens of millions of Baby Boomers adds up to a colossal chunk of discretionary time. Over a trillion days. And we'll never get that back.

As you near or enter your retirement, you will need to probe more deeply than ever into the possibilities and opportunities for a fulfilling and meaningful mature life. The biggest question retirement poses is not: What can I do? Given what has been happening to the second half of our lives, the fundamental questions now seem to be: Who do I want to become? How should I design my life? How can the second half give meaning to the whole of my life?

These are questions for people who are waking up to new possibilities after fifty. They open up vistas of purpose and untapped potential, and they lead to redefinition of retirement. The stories in Part Two will show you how pioneers have been reinventing themselves by developing rich, complex third age life portfolios and third age careers in turbulent times.

WHAT'S DIFFERENT ABOUT OUR SITUATION?

THIS CENTURY STARTED OFF like a slowly erupting volcano. After a false warning about chaos in cyberspace, with entry into the twenty-first century the global economy fell apart; in a flash investment and pension funds were decimated. Suddenly, Americans nearing retirement became anxious about diminishing resources and reduced possibilities for dream fulfillment. As one woman told us, "I was about to turn in my retirement request to Human Resources, when the value of my retirement fund dropped dramatically. I don't know anyone more ready and less prepared to retire than me. It's disheartening." Along with an economic implosion came greater competition in the marketplace, leading to draconian measures to downsize and restructure companies. People got pushed into early retirement without preparation or support.

The thought of retirement unsettles many of us in ways we never imagined. The downturn of the economy delivered a hard blow to people over fifty. We may have fears about not only what we'll do without work but also how we'll survive. One career counselor told us that his practice has totally changed. Now all his clients are over fifty, seeking new careers after leaving or losing jobs. Many approaching retirement have been placed in a dreadful situation by economic turbulence. It is like ending a long voyage and seeing a safe harbor on the horizon, only to be hit by a storm that destroys your mast. That's the bad side. But this economic climate change has also provided a wakeup call to all of us to start doing hard thinking about what is important in the second half of life.

A second destabilizing factor is the increase in social discontinuity, violence, and international political conflict. The playing field of our lives has become nearly unrecognizable. Traditions and social structures everywhere have been torn apart by an explosion of knowledge, technology, changing economics, national and cultural competition, and experimentation in lifestyles. Exacerbating the turbulence of vast social changes is a worldwide surge in violence. The tragedies of 9/11, international terrorism, wars of retaliation, ethnic violence, threats to democracy, and civil strife have been tearing apart once stable communities and personal lives. John Donne was right, "No man is an island." We have all been affected by these destabilizing factors swirling through our world.

When we look towards the future, the only thing reasonably predictable is that we shall continue to face enormous uncertainty. How can we design a bright future when so many dark clouds hover over us? How can we plan a legacy, so that we can believe our lives will have made a difference? We cannot plan a meaningful future apart from involvement with our community and the rest of the world. With a world in desperate straits and our personal timelines extending maybe another thirty or forty years, can we realistically imagine the rest of our lives spent on a golf course or on the beach?

This time of turbulence and turmoil calls out to those of us with half a century of life experience under our belts to contribute our values, visions, talents, and wisdom to the building of a more just, peaceful, and humane world. The future is calling us. That call is part of our challenge in designing our lives after fifty.

A third factor that complicates planning for the third age is the continued breakdown of traditional patterns of the life course. We grew up in a society in which it was expected that we would pass through predictable, age-graded stages. A general view has assumed that men went to school, got through adolescence, started work, got married, tried for promotions, started a family, had kids and then grandkids, retired, and became old. Women mostly stayed home. Life was structured. Everything in its place. But shortly before we got to the twenty-first century, a structured life was a thing of the past. People increasingly leave work to go back to school, change jobs and careers, move away from home, get divorced and remarried, experiment with new lifestyles, have several families, and wonder how to advance in careers when career ladders have been removed by corporate restructuring. In the past forty years women have made big changes in the old structure, changes that have affected all of us.

The old assumption that the life course moves upward to a peak, only to descend, is outdated. The ups and downs of our lives often resemble the graphs of a volatile stock market. Our aged-graded society is becoming one in which age is often irrelevant. As life structures we had taken for granted collapse, the question, "What next?" stirs up more confusion than clarity. The bad news is that we have more uncertainty in the course of our lives than ever. "The future ain't what it used to be," as Casey Stengel rued. But the good news is that with greater turbulence, uncertainty, and an indeterminate future we have more freedom to shape a life that can be more fulfilling than the old structures allowed for. And more reason for trying to do so.

To respond to the challenges facing you after fifty, you need a new perspective. Twenty years of research show us possibilities and potential that have not yet appeared on most life radar screens. Amid historical changes, all of us are also experiencing a change in the shape of the life course. A new life space has been opening up before aging kicks in.

History has placed us on a third age frontier that provides challenges for which most of us are unprepared. If we meet those challenges well, we can transform the whole second half of our lives. Just how we—you—might do this is what this book is about.

CHAPTER TWO

A NEW FRONTIER

Few there are that rightly understand of what great advantage it is
to blush at nothing and attempt everything.

—ERASMUS, *The Praise of Folly*

SEARCHING FOR AN ALTERNATIVE WAY
THROUGH MIDDLE AGE

OVER TWENTY YEARS AGO I (Bill) began to search for reliable insights into middle age. As a long-time student of human development, I was well aware of the complexities and stages of growth in youth and early adulthood, but I hadn't yet paid much attention to the second half of life. After passing fifty I started wondering about what was in store for me. Middle age certainly hadn't received good press. Textbooks described a process of decline into old age, which then supposedly started at sixty. The media were trumpeting midlife crises that often produced catastrophic consequences. Earlier in life most of us are driven by aspirations. But who aspires to become middle aged? It's so over the hill. And aging then appeared even worse. People observe passing the big five-oh apprehensively. At that age time becomes a scarce resource. Then, as now, birthday cards ridicule getting older, a modern version of gallows humor.

Yet for all the bad press, I wasn't experiencing what I was told to expect. Maybe I hadn't been reliably informed. I decided to make my own exploration into midlife and began a research project. I was hoping to find a more promising path through the middle years. What I didn't count on was that my project would last over twenty years.

I started by interviewing over a hundred people in their late forties and fifties. I began to meet individuals who intrigued me because they were not following the expected life course. They weren't having midlife crises, and they did not fit into the conventional mold of decline. Instead, they were creatively redesigning their middle years and having the best time of their lives. They were moving in new directions and experiencing growth and renewal. Sometimes even before peaking in life careers, they were starting on a second curve in the life course. They weren't always doing unusual things, but they were all experiencing life differently.

Their lives could be described in **R** words: *renewal, reinvention, regeneration, rediscovery, rejuvenation,* and *redirection.* I was so impressed by their unfolding lives that I became determined to learn all I could from them. Eventually, I tracked about three-dozen people for over ten years. I gained from them new insights into possibilities and opportunities for midlife and beyond.

From analyses of their stories I discovered six principles operating to initiate and sustain their impressive growth. I presented my findings and reflections in *The Third Age: Six Principles of Growth and Renewal After Forty*. After the book came out, I got in touch with most of the people in it. Some of them asked me, "Bill, have you learned anything from us that applies to your own life?" I was humbled by the question. "Yes, more than I ever expected," I have told them. In fact, my life has been transformed by the experience of knowing and studying them. I learned from them that we have alternatives to the conventional notions of middle aging. And I have learned how we can apply growth principles to accomplish an alternative that is truly desirable.

My wife Sallie and I have frequently talked about the challenges, tasks, and opportunities arising in the second half of life. The results of processing our learning have been stimulating and occasionally unsettling. A couple of years ago Sallie told me that she had come to the conclusion she must quit her senior position in a large HMO to redesign her life in order to satisfy emerging needs. Her decision caught me by surprise. "Are you sure this is the right thing to do, just when you're at the peak of your professional career?" I somewhat anxiously asked her. "Read your book!" she told me. Well, I have done so—again and again, every time I prepare for presentations and retreats. I'm learning that the new growth I wrote about can take us in directions we would never have predicted at an earlier age.

My wife, like those in the book, was getting in touch with a creative process deep within her, leading her to seek new forms of becoming, relationships, and fulfillment. Fifteen years earlier, as our kids were leaving home for college, she was able to devote herself to a career as a psychologist. Eventually she achieved leadership positions that matched her aspirations; along the way she completed a doctorate and also started a private practice. While proud of her impressive accomplishments in work, she was beginning to sense a need to redirect her life. Instead of channeling her creative energies into a career, she wanted more freedom to expand her talents and interests in other areas. At sixty she changed course, clarified and focused on her priorities, and restructured her world. She has also been leading and nudging me to take on retirement by redefining it. This task is no less daunting a challenge, I'm finding, than settling on a career. Together we have moved into a transition stage, searching for new possibilities in the way ahead.

OLD AND NEW VIEWS OF AGING

WHAT'S AHEAD IS **AGING**, a process that at first appears to be even less appealing than middle aging. Until recently, nearly everybody assumed that the life course was pretty well set to move down hill. Textbook titles captured the conventional belief: adult development and aging. According to professional judgment, development occurs through the first four or five decades and presumably stops before fifty. Then aging takes over. A leading expert in the field of aging recently confessed that before his research began he had assumed that after fifty there was no growth, only deterioration. His discovery of growth in aging people was a humbling experience.

Aging has conventionally been defined by **D** words: *difficulty, decline, deterioration, degeneration, decrement, disease, disengagement, depression, dependency,* and then the last **D** word that marks the end of the line. That traditional view is still widespread, encoded in textbooks, expert opinion, commonplace mindsets, the media, and culture. The *Encyclopedia* provides this description of human aging: "Gradual change in an organism that leads to an increased risk of weakness, disease, and death. There is a decline in biological functions and in ability to adapt. Overall effects of aging include reduced immunity, loss of muscular strength, and decline in memory and other aspects of cognition." Conferences on aging still abound with sessions that report in lugubrious detail varieties of physical and mental decline and loss. The decrement theory of aging, defined by the **D** words, is not only widely accepted, it is even promoted, especially by industries that capitalize on human frailties and failings. Growing old has been viewed as becoming impaired. We can call this view *usual aging*. But usual doesn't mean set in stone. Leaders in the field of gerontology around the world are beginning to redefine aging and indicate possibilities in the process not imagined in previous generations. Aging might not mean what you thought it did.

The experience of many older people today has been calling this usual view of aging into question. We don't all age in the same way. The population over fifty is extraordinarily diverse. Some seventy-year-olds look, think, act, and even feel like fifty-year-olds, and vice versa. Aging is not only the result of biology, but also it's a byproduct of historical forces, economic circumstances, and individual decisions. People over fifty today have options that didn't appear until thirty years ago. Although we're seeing more vibrant elders in our society, most people still associate being old with bad stuff. In a recent poll of a hundred and thirty thousand people, 80 percent viewed aging as a downer—and ten thousand of the respondents were over sixty. One task as we move forward in the life course is to take a hard look at what aging can mean to us.

A more positive view of aging began to emerge at the end of the twentieth century. In Europe studies recognized diversity within aging populations as well as great plasticity within individuals for positive development. We don't all age in the same way, nor at the same time, nor at the same pace. A pair of German scientists developed a theory of successful aging, based on human capacity to sustain optimal development in selected areas. Their research indicates that aging does not inevitably follow a prescribed course as previously believed. You have control over *how* you age, more so now than ever before. These scientists encourage us to question the usual view of aging, explore what is happening on the frontier of aging, and set our sights on a new goal of successful aging.

Soon thereafter a trail-blazing American report from a prestigious MacArthur study showed how people were finding alternatives to usual aging. The authors also called this new process *successful aging*. This study had followed people who were living vital, healthy, active, meaningful lives in their seventies and beyond. One of the authors in this pioneering study was an eighty-year-old psychologist. After examining the lifestyles of *successful agers*, the researchers claimed that the choices we make rather than heredity determine our health, vitality, and improved quality of life. Although this study places primary emphasis on maintaining good physical condition and a healthy lifestyle, it also stresses the importance of meaningful social engagement, a strong network of social support, and continued learning to sustain a high level of personal, social, and cognitive functioning. An even more recent American study has revealed a longer list of critically important traits and coping skills in people who age well in contrast to those who age badly. People can grow impressively as they get older.

Another myth-bashing study about becoming older appeared at the start of the twenty-first century. Contrary to what might be expected, a group of centenarians was leading healthy, active, interesting, satisfying lives right up to the end. Their successful adaptation to aging was often a result of their courage and determination in addressing formidable life challenges.

In short, recent research has an important message: if you *reframe* your life perspective, you can look forward to having a long, satisfying life—*if you do it right*. And "doing it right" calls for an attitudinal shift, careful life planning, some good fortune, wise choices, and taking control of your life well before you reach old age. These discoveries have smashed the logic underlying popular myths of aging. To age does not necessarily mean to lose resilience, dexterity, and health, nor does it inevitably lead to senility, boredom, disease, and dependency, and loss of biological, mental, and sexual functions. Aging does not have to be inevitably defined by the **D** words. Many of us have mistakenly equated aging with disease, and we've been learning that many diseases we have associated with aging are preventable. These studies have provided inspiring affirmation that each of us can look forward to a healthy, productive, purposeful, enjoyable old age; and they have marked a pathway of sensible choices to truly successful aging. How you grow older is largely up to you.

These positive, scientifically based assessments of old age throw a brighter light on future possibilities for the second half of life than any views that existed when I began my research. The new views challenge conventional expectations of aging that we've all acquired. Healthy, satisfying, competent adaptation to aging has become a legitimate goal after fifty. The natural life cycle is constrained by limits, but we have been learning that we can push against those limits and expand boundaries for vital, meaningful living.

Much depends on how you determine to use your mind. In exploring how the blind "see" by developing a capacity to visualize the world, the neurologist Oliver Sacks suggests that our minds can and should influence our brains. Contrary to the standard medical assumption that a cerebral cortex is programmed at birth, he has learned from blind people that each of us can tap creative potential to achieve a richer realization of our personal worlds. His discovery about the power of blind people's capacity to think, imagine, and choose applies to the experience of aging. Many of us have been blind to the possibilities in the second half of life. The challenge is to develop new perspectives and start visualizing them. You can slow down the decremental process of aging by imagining desired possibilities, mindfully developing your inherent creative resources, and changing course. We'll have more to say about this in the following chapters.

RISING LIFE EXPECTANCY

ANOTHER FACTOR NEEDS TO BE INCLUDED in rethinking the next phase in our lives. Amid profound changes in recent history, a quiet revolution has only gradually begun to register in our consciousness. People in most industrialized countries are living longer than ever. We are in fact experiencing a *longevity revolution*, a phenomenon just beginning to have dramatic, unforeseen consequences for individuals and society. As in many industrialized countries, Americans now live in an aging society, in which one out of three people is over fifty-five, the median age has jumped to thirty-nine, and the number of seniors over sixty-five will soon double and for the first time ever outnumber youth. A Nobel laureate, when asked what was the most significant achievement in the twentieth century, replied, "Greater longevity." Today's average life expectancy presents an unprecedented opportunity that should provoke you to rethink from scratch what you might expect for the second half of your life.

What difference will greater longevity make to each of us personally? And how many years have we gained? At the beginning of the twentieth century the average American lifespan extended about forty-seven years. By 2000 it had increased to over seventy-seven. That windfall represents a *thirty-year life bonus* for most of us, a gift of time we never anticipated. In Japan the average life expectancy has already reached eighty-four; some European countries come close to that average. Americans are catching up; soon the average will be over eighty. If you've completed higher education, your chances of living well into your eighties are more than double what they would be without it. Furthermore, thanks to modern medicine and insights into health and wellbeing, the life expectancies of men and women are moving towards equality. Most of us can expect to live much longer than we ever imagined. Your thirty-year life bonus should stimulate you to take another look at life after fifty and retirement.

How much longer might your life last? What do the numbers tell us? Not long ago the fastest growing segment of the population was the cohort over eighty-five. Today the fastest growing segment consists of centenarians. In 1965 America had three thousand of them, few enough that Willard Scott could wish many of them happy birthday on the *Today Show*. By the turn of the century the number had passed seventy-five thousand. In the middle of the twenty-first century millions of Americans will live past a hundred. You may be one of them. While the maximum human lifespan has so far remained constant at about a hundred and twenty years, average life expectancy continues to increase.

Recently, a demographer predicted that half the American girls born today have a reasonable chance to live a century. My colleague, the Stanford physician Wally Bortz, who has specialized in healthy, active aging, has written a challenging book, Dare to Be 100. Why not take him up on it? Your chance of living so long might be improved if you plan on it. The study of vital centenarians encourages each of us to do so. If you're fifty, you might have another fifty years in front of you. At sixty you could have half your adult life ahead of you. Imagine that!

What will you do with this gift of life? If we develop a new perspective, take good care of ourselves, and make good use of medical science, we're likely to live much longer than previous generations. The biggest challenge is how we can make the *more* years ahead of us *better*. The research cited above indicates how we can age well and promote successful aging during our last two decades. But what about the two or three decades before that? My research focuses on a largely overlooked middle period that has opened up because of the longevity revolution, modern medicine, and social changes.

This new period radically changes the landscape of the life course. Another radical change reshaped the early part of the life course a hundred years ago. A brief transition from childhood to adulthood through puberty was transformed by economic, political, educational, and social factors into a new life stage called adolescence. You won't read about teenagers in the fiction of Hawthorne, Melville, or Twain. Adolescence hadn't arrived yet. Something similar is now taking place in our middle years. At this point in history those of us over fifty are entering a third age frontier. What does this frontier mean to the second half of our lives?

IS AGING THE ONLY OPTION?

JIM AND I FEEL AS ENCOURAGED by recent discoveries about greater life expectancy and successful aging as anyone. Who doesn't want to live long and age well? "Live long and pros-per," in the words of Mr. Spock of *Star Trek*. Yet for all the pos-itive qualities in the new view of aging, the focus has been on life after seventy-five, the *fourth age*. It seems to us that the suc-cessful aging scenario represents more of a holding pattern than significant growth. Successful aging recognizes the dete-rioration inevitable in old age and recommends adaptation by selecting behaviors to compensate for physical decline. Successful aging thus resembles damage control, not growth. Aging suggests subtraction; growth implies addition. In the third age we need to apply a different kind of math.

Suppose we have another option. The fourth age is an age for completion. What about the third quarter and the thirty-year life bonus? What difference can that make? How has it been accounted for? Aging studies often skip over it. If we want to be truly inventive, we might ask: where will we experience this bonus? At the end? Or before the end? In my research I have seen people living a paradox of growth and aging in the third age. Their lives are not so much shaped by limiting forces as driven by a creative power different from the energy of successful aging. As the Dutch translation of *The Third Age* suggested, this new period can be a time of blos-soming. Your life after fifty can be a time for experimentation and fulfillment.

When talking with people who have read *The Third Age*, I've asked, "What was the most important thing you got from it?" One of the most reassuring responses has been, "I learned that I have options. I had assumed that life after fifty was pretty much prescribed—downhill all the way. Now I know that doesn't have to happen. I have choices." They have been encouraged to take the road less traveled. You, too, can change course and navigate in a way few have done so far—*and that will make all the difference.* It's your decision.

THE DAWN OF A NEW THIRD AGE

To UNDERSTAND AND APPRECIATE THIS EMERGING FRONTIER, we need fresh terms so that we do not become bogged down by conventional, enervating assumptions about becoming older. One reason we get locked into the old paradigm of aging is because we lack the language to describe alternatives. It's hard to see something if we can't name it. And it's harder yet to say something different with a limited, worn out vocabulary. I like a phrase commonly used in Europe, Canada, and Australia, the *third age*. The term is catching on in America. In other countries the third age usually refers to retirement. To us it signifies something much more significant.

This term is virtually free of the stereotypes and limiting expectations generally attached to middle age and aging. Because the term is so new to Americans, it generates questions; and that can be a start of opening our minds. It has generally meant the period between second age activities and the fourth age. In other countries it has often been seen as a time for retirees to be involved in lifelong learning, promoted by programs such as third age universities.

For us the third age signifies a change in the life structure, a revolution that provides an opportunity to transform aging and experience fulfillment. It designates a new landscape in the life course, from fifty to the late seventies, even early eighties. As more and more people realize the potential offered by the third age, we are likely to see a change in our country to support alternative life options after fifty. The time is now ripe to start making changes in our culture, institutions, work and retirement policies, and lifestyles.

In our society people have generally focused on the second age. We now spend the first quarter century of our lives preparing for it. The common measures of success have been based on second age achievements in work, family, finances, hobbies, and community. Today's cultural heroes are for the most part recognized for what they do or have done in their second age. There's a cultural lag between what we can become in the third age and the stereotypes of people over fifty. Negative images still abound in the workplace, the media, advertisements, birthday cards, and jokes about aging. Often contrary ideas such as our message evoke glassy-eyed stares. Invest to develop people in their fifties and sixties? That notion still seems too fanciful to be taken seriously.

In spite of emerging signs of vitality in people over fifty, most of us do not yet have an adequate sense of the new frontier ahead of us. A fulfilling third age is just not on our life maps. We all need to question our own life maps and the road we're traveling. Do you see the road ahead as a cul-de-sac? Or is it a fork in the road? Or is it off the road? Do you want to settle down or change course? The pioneers in our research show that the third age offers paths to fulfillment other generations could never have imagined. It's time to empty the trash in our subconscious and draw new life maps. The English poet Robert Browning's poem "Rabbi Ben Ezra" (1864) was way ahead of its time. The Rabbi proclaims:

Grow old along with me!
The best is yet to be,
The last of life, for which the first was made.

That sentiment represents a discovery about life after fifty, an insight that we are just beginning to catch up with. A scientist once observed, "Discovery consists of seeing what everybody has seen and thinking what nobody else has thought." What are you thinking?

THE OPTION OF SECOND GROWTH

THE PEOPLE IN OUR RESEARCH have been showing how to develop what I've called *second growth*. In making presentations about this new possibility, I have sometimes encountered skepticism. Are these people really so different? "Show us!" audiences have sometimes seemed to tell me. One woman who has manifested prodigious growth for over thirty years was the subject of a documentary that I have been able to show in presentations.

Daphne, whose story fills nearly half of chapter 8 in *The Third Age*, caught my attention when her achievement of a Ph.D. at seventy was reported in the newspapers. When I interviewed her, she told me how she had experienced liberation by reading Betty Friedan's *The Feminine Mystique* during her forties. As a single mom with three kids, she developed a successful career as a decorator. Years of psychotherapy helped her discover core values and elements of her personality that she wanted to affirm. In her early fifties she won a grant to study indigenous arts and crafts in Indian villages; her nearly two-year stay influenced her development even more. Returning to the States, she balanced commitments to daily exercise, environmental preservation, her grown children, a new relationship, and a wide circle of friends with an emerging learning project. She started a research project into vital aging, concluding with her doctoral dissertation.

The documentary on Daphne reveals a seventy-six-year-old woman blossoming in second growth—active in a dance class, hiking with women in an Idaho wilderness, entertaining friends with music, dancing, and elegant dining, traveling to exotic places with her partner, teaching in a college classroom, and reflecting on the meaning of aging. "That vibrant woman is seventy-six?" people ask. "She seems younger than my parents, who are in their sixties," adult students have told me. She illustrates the genuine possibility of second growth through a long third age. Skeptical faces have melted into admiration. Daphne turned eighty-four as I was writing this chapter; in her fourth age she exemplifies successful aging. She had returned from a two-month visit to India, was preparing to give a presentation at an aging conference in Italy, and was writing a book about vital aging. Like the others you will read about in this book, her sustained growth after fifty has been breaking the mold of aging.

Second growth represents a new option in the life course. This growth process differs from growth at an earlier age. Second growth is not a linear add-on process, but more complex and paradoxical; and it requires much inner work. At its core second growth taps and expresses the creative potential that has often lain dormant, or even been repressed earlier. A second harvest in our lives reaps the output of creativity that may not have been ready to be tapped in the first half of life. Second growth in the third age also suggests how retirement can become a time for freedom, creativity, and purpose. Redefining retirement can set the stage for you to create the person you've always wanted to become.

In the third age we should be keen to redirect our course inward to tap buried potential, enabling us to be freer in moving outward. Our emphasis changes from extrinsic achievements to inherently worthwhile endeavors such as exploring, creating, becoming, connecting, and giving. Getting in touch with your inner core is like finding an old attic trunk filled with things you've forgotten, discarded, or ignored in your adult years. This new growth will enable you to recycle many of your talents and express them in new forms. Give yourself permission to unpack elements that in your second age you had neither appreciation nor time for. As a sixty-year-old former executive in a third age retreat expressed it:

> The whole first half of my life was geared to being a successful achiever. When I was in school and then throughout my career, I had clear, firm goals. Now that I have left my corporate position I'm discovering aspects of myself that I never developed. My hope is that I can be much better balanced, and be more in touch with emotions, family, friends, and a spirit of play that I didn't have time for.

He and his wife, a physician, have been designing a different kind of life than they had during their second age careers. And the youth in him is delighted with a new motorcycle that literally takes him down roads less traveled! Another businessman who has been developing third age awareness, recently commented, "I'm experiencing at this time in my life a wide-open space that gives me a sense of freedom that is exhilarating. I'm getting beyond a fairly rigid sequence in life to realize a freedom to be myself, to be more authentic."

These people have begun to cash in early on the thirty-year bonus, while still developing new careers. Their second growth represents a creative organizing principle for their lives after fifty, and it lays a foundation for successful aging in the fourth age. Like them, you can also discover and create a vital alternative for your second half of life, using the six principles we'll explore in the next chapter.

CHAPTER THREE

PRINCIPLES OF THIRD AGE GROWTH AND RENEWAL

What lies behind us, and what lies before us,
are tiny matters compared to what lies within us.

—EMERSON

HOW DO WE CHANGE COURSE?

PUZZLED BY THE STORIES I WAS HEARING when I started this research twenty years ago, I kept asking myself: what are these people doing to initiate and sustain their remarkable growth? After years of sifting through transcripts, a quantitative analysis, and reflection, I realized that all of them engage in soul-searching questioning about themselves, their lives, and their future. Here are questions I've heard people raise, inquiries that have shaped the second half of their lives:

- What do I value most? What's most important?

- What do I really want in life? What's my next adventure?

- What should I let go of now? What do I want to keep?
- How can I have more fun? What's my passion?
- In my journey so far, what have I suppressed? What have I missed?
- How can I recover or add missing pieces to my life?
- How and where will I find meaning and purpose in the second half of life?
- What kind of person do I want to become?
- What will replace the everyday joys of raising children?
- What can I do to fill the void created when children move away?
- How can I find new ways to nurture both others and myself?
- What's holding me back? How can I overcome these obstacles?
- How can I achieve integrity? How can I develop spiritually?
- What difference will my life make? What legacy do I want to leave?

Many tough questions surface as we take stock of our lives. They don't arise in any given order or in exactly these words. One probing question leads to another and then another, fostering a complex ongoing process. A series of such questions can release enormous creative energy.

Raising these questions prompts an inner dialogue, what I've called *mindful reflection*. This way to use our minds is an ability that differs from what most of us are used to. Since school days we have been sharpening the skill of analytical problem solving. That ability has enabled us to clarify goals, detect obstacles, and clear them away to get ahead. This linear, left-brain operation works fine for many things. But to change course we have to call on the power of imagination and use our right brains to reflect on how we'd like our personal worlds to shape up as we grow older. To get our creative juices flowing, we need to dream more.

Mindful reflection taps the creative resources churning in deep reservoirs in our minds, clarifies options, and helps us prioritize them. As we visualize what could be, we have to make choices, sometimes trying things we've never dared. Mindful reflection by itself isn't enough. It needs to be joined with a willingness to experiment and take risks. This complex, paradoxical inner process represents the first principle in second growth.

In questioning their lives, these people have also become critically aware of what I've called *old scripts*, well-entrenched assumptions that are obstacles to change and growth. We all have old scripts—outworn ideas, expectations, habitual responses, fears, and blindspots—buried in our subconscious. Each of us has to recognize, challenge, and revise the old scripts associated with aging, because these predispositions send us erroneous messages about growing older. Most of us have not learned to age well.

Many of us have internalized dreadful examples of aging from previous generations. These stereotypical assumptions and expectations of what lies ahead are unsuitable to the changing landscape of our lives. In workshops and retreats

I have become more convinced than ever that raising awareness of old scripts is an indispensable part of the first principle. Like rewriting a document, we first have to delete old material. Old scripts have programmed us to stay in place or retreat instead of inspiring us to dream of new possibilities. What makes it even more difficult is that we live in a society that idolizes youth and the second age. Don't you think that American culture makes it difficult to see the value of being older? Powerful cultural symbols in the media suggest that the only people who count are thirty and under. The media bombard us with caricatures of old people, purportedly comic images that would be funny were they not so outrageous.

Pre-industrial cultures venerated elders, listened to them, and were guided by them. Our culture generates a dismal view of aging that is insulting, patronizing, and debilitating. In society and the workplace ageism remains widespread and oppressive. Stereotypes of aging often get implanted in our brains and undermine our development by becoming the working assumptions, or mental models, that shape our thinking and behavior. If we're going to free ourselves from these stereotypes, we need to identify and shred our own old scripts.

In addition to having to overcome stereotypes of aging, we are all creatures of habit. Most of us have become comfortable with an adult identity and customary ways of thinking and acting. It's easy to freeze up and become stuck with your habitual, second age self. Middle age stagnation has become a common malady. How can you become unstuck? To move out of your comfort zone, you have to learn to let go. Watching a program illustrating how actors in training get freed up to release creativity suggests how any of us can tap the potential to step outside habitual responses and behaviors. Young actors put on masks and become the person represented by the mask. The mask challenges and frees them to be different. With a different face actors can overcome inhibitions, drop habitual presentation of themselves, and perform in surprising new ways. They discover new talents, traits, and gestures as they reinvent themselves. The people in the research underlying both books have been doing something similar, not with masks but in new settings. Many have stepped outside of usual roles by putting themselves in a different situation, like taking a sabbatical, going on a retreat, spending time in the wilderness, participating in a mind opening program or counseling, or taking a break from everyday routine with a good friend with whom it is safe to explore options. Mindfulness, as Harvard psychologist Ellen Langer has shown, can be promoted by putting ourselves in a different context. One man told me,

> I was so caught up in the corporate mold—even after I retired. I'm enjoying pulling way back from the corporate environment and rediscovering who I am without it. Only now can I see with clarity how far into it I went and how much of myself I left unused while I was there. It took relocation and experiencing months of confusion to shed the imprinting of thirty years before I sensed an unfolding of who I really am.

In a different context people have found freedom to challenge both cultural and self-imposed obstacles to growth and try out new selves with altered behaviors. It's not only habits of doing that need breaking; you need to change your perspective and how you think about your unfolding life. A driving question emerges: how can you reframe your future so that you can experience the results you truly desire? That's where the six principles of growth and renewal come in.

SIX PRINCIPLES OF GROWTH AND RENEWAL

THE SIX PRINCIPLES THAT OPERATE in the unfolding lives of people who manifest second growth represent a major discovery about new growth after fifty. These paradoxical principles operate in the people whose stories fill both *The Third Age* and *Changing Course*. Consider the principles as checkpoints for your journey as you engage in third age planning:

- Practicing mindful reflection and risk taking;

- Developing realistic optimism;

- Creating a positive third age identity;

- Balancing greater freedom with deeper, more intimate relationships;

- Redefining and balancing work and play; and,

- Caring for others, earth, and self.

We cannot offer a formula for embracing and practicing these principles. The principles contain paradoxes requiring each of us to juggle intentions that on the surface seem to contradict each other. Each of us has to personalize our own growth. Yet this simple list can help you become conscious of your third age potential and of the areas that need your attention.

As you start the process with mindful reflection and risk taking, you will need another principle. Buttressing the whole process is the indispensable quality of realistic optimism. A pessimistic, defeatist attitude will not inspire you to search for a new way. Although a few of the people I've focused on are congenital optimists, most of us have to work on developing a grownup optimism that embraces realism. Many people I've interviewed have told stories of setbacks and tragedies that have nevertheless concluded with acts of resilience and renewal. Some have been undone with grief. "What did you do when you got knocked down?" I asked them. Usually they told me that they had turned to good friends and counselors to help them heal and reframe a new, positive perspective. Friends can help you form a personal vision of what can be, combined with a truthful awareness of rough spots, dangers, and losses.

You need encouragement to face realistically your uncertain future and vulnerability. And you need to affirm control of your life with a perspective saturated with hope and self-confidence. As I showed in my last book, realistic optimism is an important growth principle that can be learned. It motivates and encourages us to explore fresh possibilities and risk reaching out for them.

The first two principles of growth and renewal set the foundation for changing course after fifty. They apply to four areas of life: 1) an evolving personal identity; 2) work, play, and retirement; 3) expanding personal freedom and intimate relationships; and, 4) an enlarged sphere of caring. Before exploring how people have been applying these principles, let's see how one woman got under way.

HOW THE FIRST TWO PRINCIPLES GET US STARTED

Whenever I have addressed audiences about third age growth, I have found an upbeat response to the story of Professor Lin from *The Third Age*. Her experience illustrates clearly and dramatically how this process unfolds, because I could see it happening in her life. Early in my research a contingent of Chinese scholars arrived for a sabbatical at the university where I was teaching. I became acquainted with the leader of this group, a woman whom I guessed to be nearing sixty. During the fall semester, I noticed changes in her appearance and behavior. She had shed her drab gray outfit and was wearing colorful blouses and tweed skirts. Often her walk across campus left young students trailing behind. When I visited her class on Chinese language and culture, I observed a dynamic teacher interacting with students with sharp comments and pointed humor. While on sabbatical, she seemed to be blossoming. I knew I had to learn more from her. I was sure she could help me better understand how second growth can get under way.

In my first interview, Professor Lin told me of her life in China. As a student she had believed firmly in Mao's political philosophy and committed herself to the betterment of her country. After obtaining a graduate degree in science, she earned another degree in Russian. She worked for a science journal in her university. At thirty she was thrilled with her career. She married another scientist, and soon they had two children. All went well until the Cultural Revolution shattered nearly everything she had worked for. She had a terribly hard time, and many of her friends died. She felt she had been robbed of ten years. After the revolution she returned to the university, where she eventually took a job teaching English to Chinese students.

When I asked her how she felt about her life now, her response was tinged with remorse. She felt herself getting older and her abilities fading. She said she envied the younger generation as good times were returning to China. In her early comments she seemed like an aging woman in decline, too old for promising development. Old scripts were still operating. Yet, I had started to notice that other side. What was she experiencing during this yearlong sabbatical? She made a particularly significant comment:

> While I have been in America, I have forgotten my age. If I were in China, there would be so many things that would remind me of my age. Here, nothing reminds me of how old I am. The secretary even refers to us as 'girls.' My life here has allowed me to study as much as I want, to learn, to communicate openly with many people, and to wear what I want. In China I would not wear bright colors like this. Here, older people can wear colorful clothing, but in China people my age wear only gray, brown, or blue.

Her sabbatical had presented Professor Lin an unexpected opportunity. Placing herself in a different context from everyday constraints, obligations, and expectations freed her to discover hidden potential. She escaped the old Chinese scripts for elderly people and experienced liberation, a chance to let go of habits and rediscover suppressed qualities. She felt free to experiment with a new lifestyle. She found in this American sabbatical an opportunity to explore new possibilities about herself, to reject old scripts, to develop vital skills and interests, and to change her perspective and lifestyle. Contrary to her own conventional expectations, she was initiating unexpected new growth at fifty-six. In launching a new direction for her life, she was also recovering an optimistic spirit, what Chinese call a *sunny view*. She was visibly excited by this new start. For me, her transformation indicated a radically different possibility, a second chance for growth and renewal in the second half of life. Later, she made an observation that signaled a sea change in her development:

I feel like I'm getting my youth back. Here, I look younger, feel younger. I'm starting to become more courageous. I used to fear making mistakes. Now I am taking more risks. Coming here was a risk. When I return, I cannot imagine retiring, staying home, and giving up on vigorous activities. I am becoming more open—more open to people and to possibilities in myself. I'm more optimistic and feel much more in control of my life than I did ten years ago. My goal when I go home is to continue what I've started.

Professor Lin is one of dozens of people who have shown how to break the mindlessness of conventional notions about what to expect and how to start a new creative process of growth through the third age. What did she do?

- She became more aware of the full scope of her personality and hidden potential;

- She critically questioned and started letting go of old scripts and society's expectations of her;

- She clarified her values and visualized what she really wanted to do and become, rejecting the prospects of idle retirement and premature old age;

- She set long-term goals and took risks to reach them;

- She became more optimistic about her life chances; and,

- She developed a new self-image and assumed more control over her life.

Like other people I've been tracking, she has been taking these steps to realize Rabbi Ben Ezra's promise, "The best is yet to be."

THE PIVOTAL PRINCIPLE:
BUILDING A POSITIVE THIRD AGE IDENTITY

WHEN I WROTE **THE THIRD AGE**, I listed the task of building a new identity as one of the six principles of growth and renewal. I have since realized that this principle forms the core of second growth. Its importance has not yet been adequately recognized in mature adult development and most books about aging. Writers on the subject seem to assume that by the time you've grown up your identity is well established. In the first half of life a major task was to forge a personal identity that nourishes self-esteem and serves as a guide for choices and behavior. As a child, major chunks of your identity were issued to you in terms of race, ethnicity, gender, appearance, locations, and family position. As you grew up, your identity became more individualized by your behavior, personality, relationships, and achievements. Your second age adult identity has largely been forged by the roles you have played in a variety of institutions, such as family, work, and community. Achieving this identity has been hard work. You can be proud of it.

Yet, the identity you developed during second age is inappropriate for life after fifty, because your relationships to many key institutions have changed. And because after a half-century of living you're ready for an identity change as you begin to address other issues. Each of us has an identity that has been waiting in the wings, a new self that will prompt each of us to become a different, more complete person in the third age. For some people a nascent awareness of an *ideal self* begins to call for a new identity. A former bank executive described how he decided to take an early retirement at fifty-two so that he could affirm a suppressed self by developing a new career in the public sector.

I had been with the bank for over twenty-five years and was beginning to realize that what the bank was expecting of me didn't fit well with what I was expecting of me. I saw that this conflict would only intensify if I stayed. I was becoming more conscious of a basic value of public service that had been dormant as I rose up the career ladder. My decision to leave the bank was primarily to give me a chance to follow that value and contribute to the nonprofit sector. I've been lucky, because my new career in nonprofits has been rewarding, allowing me to become more like the person I really want to be.

His change of course started a growth process that has surprised him. During the past fifteen years he has become freer to become *the person he wants to be*, rather than maintain the persona the bank and society seemed to demand.

This kind of self-awareness moves us towards a post-institutional identity in the third age. Many career women and men approaching and entering retirement have discovered that in this significant transition they need to develop new, more personal and individualized self-images. In transition, what happens to our sense of self as we step out of our primary career? Most of us have worked hard through the second age to establish an identity that has largely been defined by career achievements.

For many of us, our whole lives have been geared to this end. As children, we were constantly asked, "What do you want to be when you grow up?" The expected answer was some kind of a job or career. In the second age, when you met someone new, how did you identify yourself? Most likely, you mentioned where you spent most of your time: in work and in the family. As we grow older, we need to reframe the question and the answer. What kind of person do you want to become in your third age? What does your ideal self look like? Where is the life you are building now taking you? Through your transition into the second half of life, you should keep these questions alive.

Especially in pre-retirement planning it's a good idea to think mindfully about developing a freestanding post-institutional identity, one that transcends conventional roles to affirm the person you can become. A surgeon commented that this kind of transcendence demands shifting gears by raising a different question: "For the past thirty years I have been committed to being the best doctor I can be. How can I be the best? I still want that. But I'm now widening my scope and asking: how can I become a whole person? That's what I need to work on next."

This work has gradually led him to redesign his life during his sixties so that he has more balanced commitments among career, marriage, family, community service, and free time. Like others in my study, he has realized that the person he wants to be when he "grows up" is more fulfilled, complex, and complete. Shaping a positive identity to become a whole person, to move towards an ideal self, is a vital task for all of us for as long as we live. It can even add years to our lives. A Yale University study of elderly people in a community in Ohio discovered that those who had a positive image of themselves in aging lived seven and a half years longer than those with a negative self-image. No one can guarantee that reinventing yourself will extend your life; it might. But I have become convinced that it's crucial to improving the quality of our lives as we grow older.

Over and over in interviews I've heard people saying that as they were *changing course*, a major goal emerges: "To become the person I can be." Many have related that they were experiencing freedom from the pull of conventional expectations, external achievements, and status symbols to explore other interests and untapped potential. People growing through the third age become more inner-directed. At least in modern Western cultures there seems to be a natural progression in life, moving from a life centered on achievement and external recognition to one aimed at fulfillment.

The result of inner, reflective dialogue leads to a complex self, integrating qualities and intentions that got short shrift in second age. Often with pride and a deep sense of satisfaction, the people from whom I've been learning lay aside a former identity to explore aspects and opportunities that have been suppressed. They often discover their personal worlds expanding. In a third age retreat, Lee, a fifty-year-old businessman, told us, "I feel like I've been getting back qualities from my youth. In thirty years of work I lost that. My world was shrinking. I flew over two hundred thousand miles, but my world was small. This past year, I haven't been anywhere, but my world is larger."

People like Lee are finding a true self that has been ignored or lost in the pursuit of external success. Letting go in this manner requires both courage and financial resources. Depending on your finances, you may be able at this time to let go of only certain aspects of your second age identity. You can most likely let go of more than you believe you can. Let your courage drive you, but have enough sense *not* to let it drive you into the ground. But, a start is a start.

Jack, the idiosyncratic college president in *The Third Age*, first retired in his late fifties to head a nonprofit institution, and then he retired again when he was sixty-five to buy and start operating an inn in Vermont. This venture marked the realization of a dream he had long suppressed; he named it *The Inn at Long Last*. At seventy he wrote that his life was coming together in an integrated whole. When he was seventy-five, he changed again, moving on to purchase and operate a small-town newspaper. This former economist talked about his unfolding self like a psychologist. "We all have sides to us that need to be discovered and brought out. You do, too," he told me when he was thinking about leaving the inn. Old standards, titles, and roles become less important as we journey through the second half of life towards mature self-realization. A participant in a third age retreat put it this way:

> When I introduced myself at the opening, I didn't mention anything about my thirty-year career with the company. Near the end, I worked my way up to become an executive vice president. I was proud of that. I've wondered why I didn't say anything about it. I was right not to. That position is not relevant to where I am with my life now and what's important to me at this stage. I didn't retire, I graduated, and that means commencement of a whole new development.

Similarly, in a totally different context from her everyday life in China, Professor Lin was beginning to realize that she had so much more vitality, creativity, and talent than cultural expectations assumed. Like masked actors, she was breaking away from the rules and roles that had constrained her identity, blossoming in ways that surprised her. Like others in this study, she found increased freedom an opportunity to develop a distinctive, mature identity that stands on its own. A maxim that suits our quest on the new frontier comes from Morrie Schwarz, the amazing professor who while dying bravely encouraged us all, "We should be looking at our potential, stretching ourselves into everything we can become." Now that's a motto for second growth!

WHAT ARE KEY IDENTITY ISSUES
IN THIRD AGE AND RETIREMENT?

WHERE DOES THIS **STRETCH** REACH? Creating a positive third age identity involves addressing important issues, some perhaps for the first time. These matters include: viewing ourselves as mature adults while rediscovering youthful traits; tapping creative and emotional depths; developing a healthy lifestyle for optimal wellbeing; redefining success; modifying our understanding of gender; redefining and balancing work and play; revaluing and strengthening our most important relationships; nurturing spirituality; and clarifying what we most care about, what kind of legacy we want to leave, and what contributions we can make to the future. Consider any one of these items.

- How does your view of yourself today and the promise of your life now compare to what you held and practiced ten years ago?

- How do you see your life changing in the next five years?

- What do you need to do to come up with answers that will satisfy you?

Unsettling questions like these emerge, especially when we think about the future in retirement.

REDEFINING SUCCESS

When you retire, how will you measure your success? Most people I have followed have been successful in both personal and conventional terms. During the second age you have achieved goals and filled roles that have brought satisfaction, recognition, and meaning. But how can you see your life as successful in the third age as you move into retirement, especially if you buy into its traditional definition as not-working? Does success apply only to your past? As a former senior manager put it, "How are you supposed to transition from being somebody to being some nobody?" That topic doesn't appear yet in programs for conventional retirement planning.

Some people apparently can't find an answer and refuse to retire. They are afraid to let go. One man approaching seventy, who has been successful in several careers, when asked about retirement, replied, "I have no plans to retire. It scares the hell out of me. I just hope to keep working here until they carry me out in ten or twenty years." To get beyond this fear each of us needs to redefine success. We shouldn't accept retirement as *becoming a nobody.*

All the ideas and markers most of us have used to define success were formulated under a different set of rules. For decades we have assumed specific roles that identified who we are; and we've had fairly obvious measures to tell us how successful we've been: income, position, status, achievement, recognition, parenting, community leadership, service, and so on. When jobs are over and kids have left home, what roles are left? Who are we when the roles run out? The roles gave us purpose, direction, goals, and rewards. They provided a framework of success that was perhaps right for the second age. This framework is still assumed to be definitive—in spite of so much life after retiring, it's used to write most obituaries. Second age accomplishments supposedly tell the world who we were after we've left. Where in this perspective do we find meaningful success beyond the second age? Do we still share the common assumption that the best things in life occur before we're fifty?

In Western culture we tend to view our lives in linear fashion, measuring points along the way with birthdays, anniversaries, and other external markers. We become obsessed with doing. Our fear of retirement expresses itself in the question: what shall I do with all this empty, unstructured time? Other cultures have been better at appreciating the uneven patterns and inner paradoxes in the life course. The Japanese, for example, chart the journey across life in terms of perfecting one's inner nature. They call it *kokoro*. To them, merely *doing* is meaningless unless a person is able to become deeper and wiser along the way. But even the Japanese, I'm told, are having trouble these days with retirement. Perhaps like those of us in Western cultures, they too have been modernized. Developing our inner nature to become a whole person seems to be a lesson we can all learn.

Building a new identity of which we can be proud calls for recasting the standards by which we assess our journey. It means moving beyond second age notions of success. That often-painful transition calls for both letting go of former measures that were once so important and nurturing new dreams. This transition beats at the heart of the creative process of reinventing ourselves in the third age. Ben Zander, conductor of the Boston Philharmonic Orchestra, tells how he transformed the "success game" into a new one called I *am a contribution.* "Throw yourself into life as someone who makes a difference," he writes. See yourself as a contribution.

The psychologist Mihaly Csikszentmihalyi, on the other hand, advocates redefining our life goal in terms of increasing the *flow* in our lives. Flow represents optimal experience, when we do what we love and develop our full potential. People whose growth has so impressed me have been recasting success. They are not straining to move a notch higher, but tapping their unique potential to become the person they can be, realizing a vision of becoming, sharing, caring, and happiness. "How do you view your life now?" I always ask them. "It's never been better," is the answer I usually hear. They are putting more flow into their lives. They haven't left success behind them; they've transformed it.

REASSESSING YOUR AGE: GROWING OLDER/GROWING YOUNG

Building a positive third age identity also calls for upside-down thinking about age. How do you feel about your age? And how do you feel about openly admitting it? Growing older in a youth-fixated culture can be hazardous to your wellbeing, not to mention your sanity. In simpler societies becoming old was welcomed as a gain; it signified the prime of life. For our society it's seen as a loss. Age does not imply value added for people, as it usually does for antiques and fine red wine. Some of us are tempted to lie about our age, and many try to deny our years. As one man told me, "I just can't believe I'm as old as the guy I shave every morning." An attractive seventy-year-old woman reluctantly said, "I'll tell you my age. But you mustn't publish it."

New industries are making fortunes supporting people's wishes to defy aging by denying it. Everything we know about wholesome adaptation tells us that the age denial we see in modern cultures is unhealthy. Denial sets us off in a wrong direction. In forming an appropriate identity, each of us needs to come to terms with her or his own age. But that acknowledgment doesn't mean classifying yourself as old, worn out, ossified, or decrepit. Older can mean *better*.

Many people seem to be younger in midlife than their parents. Several aspects of modern society, such as education, information about nutrition, regular exercise, and a cultural scrambling of typical age norms, have apparently slowed the aging process for many people. As one woman told me, "I'm fifty-five now and feel that life is better than ever. I see wonderful possibilities ahead of me. But my mother at this age already had one foot in the grave." Many of us are unsure what it means to be a certain age today. That's healthy. The great baseball pitcher Satchel Paige asked, "How old would you be if you didn't know how old you was?" When I ask that question, I hear comments like this, "I'm sixty-three, but when I close my eyes I feel that I'm about forty-five." In chapter 6 you will read Faye's story and her rhetorical question, "How am I supposed to feel at sixty?" Rethinking age involves living the paradox of growing older/growing young.

The term *growing young* suggests an important task that is a healthy alternative to denial. It doesn't signify the defying of aging. The anthropologist Ashley Montagu invented the term *neotony* to account for a human trait that has contributed to successful survival in evolution. It means to hold youthful characteristics. Unlike other primates, humans retain youthful physical features throughout their lives. Montagu suggested that in adulthood we live and grow successfully if we hold (or recover) youthful traits, such as curiosity, spontaneity, imagination, laughter, and playfulness. Our goal, he said, is "to grow young and to die young as late as possible."

Psychologists who have talked about nurturing an inner child have been suggesting a similar point. In developing our identities during the second age, many of us have often suppressed youthful qualities as we assumed greater responsibilities. Now you have the chance to back up and recover wonderful traits left behind. The pursuit of fame, fortune, and security often buries childhood qualities. The third age gives us all an opportunity to recover youthful qualities to use on the voyage. In his autobiography the psychologist Jerome Bruner wrote that in his later years he was learning to recover the boy within him and give him more speaking parts in his life. People have told me they feel that they are getting their youth back. For others who may feel in some ways that they were shortchanged during childhood, the third age represents newfound opportunity to express themselves. One fifty-seven-year-old woman remarked, "I can now do what I feared to do as a shy child."

People grow young by bringing a youthful spirit back into their lives and by putting more emphasis on play, having fun, and laughter. Second age achievement involves serious work. In the third age we are freer to let go of a compulsive pursuit of external success. It helps to let a little Zen into our lives: *Don't just do something. Sit there!* We become more mindful as we realize that each moment is precious. We can use an increase in freedom to practice the childlike art of *being here* now. The sixty-three-year-old who feels forty-five withdrew from the corporate world to follow a creative passion and dedicates part of his life to helping young people learn the value of appreciating the wilderness and conserving nature. Out in the woods he experiences a youthful passion.

Many people have also brought youthfulness back into their lives by developing a much healthier, more active lifestyle than they had in the second age. Ironically, news in the media report that Americans are increasingly at risk because of poor diets, overeating and obesity, and inactivity, not to mention smoking and the abuse of drugs and alcohol. Yet many third agers are jettisoning bad health habits, learning about nutrition, engaging in regular exercise, and trying out challenging activities. Many of those in this study have reported they are in better physical shape at sixty than they were at forty or fifty. I have been surprised to discover so many women and men over sixty going to training centers several times a week for vigorous workouts. Many are also becoming actively involved in the outdoors, breaking from a sedentary lifestyle. They hike, jog, bike, swim, kayak, sail, ski, play tennis, and golf—carrying their clubs—on a regular basis. As they become living examples of the paradox of *vital aging*, they are having more fun after sixty than they did in the first half of life.

Another paradox further complicates this process of growing older/growing young. Appreciation of renewed vitality and greater happiness needs to be set in the context a whole life, meaning that we need consciously to raise our awareness of our mortality. We have a chance to live much longer today. But a thirty-year life bonus is not immortality. We are growing older. With heightened awareness we can sense precious moments that hover like rainbows, gracing our lives. But these moments pass; we shall, too. Acknowledging the end helps us become grateful for the gift of being alive. I have regularly asked people in this study, "How does awareness of your mortality affect you?" Invariably I have heard, "Knowing I will die encourages me to make the most of my life now." They are not strangers to death. All have lost loved ones—parents, best friends, and even children. A few have had a life-threatening illness.

In contrast to fear of death that purportedly sets off midlife crises, the pioneers on the frontier of the third age have been stretching their scope in two directions: back to youthful qualities and forward to their end. They are learning to see life "whole." The result is renewed gratitude for life and a richer appreciation of the present.

REDEFINING GENDER

The challenge to rethink what age means becomes particularly poignant as we reassess gender. What does it mean to become an older woman, an older man? Adding "older" to a sense of gender has the effect of diminishing returns. We fear that in this vital area of our identities, we're losing it. The media add insult to injury with unflattering portraits of men and women over fifty. New industries exploit fears by promising to hide telltale signs and restore the qualities of youth. Damage control. Dream creams, lotions and potions, pills for thrills, tonics and bionics, dyes and dips, hair transplants and facelifts. Gizmos and tricks and voodoo to turn back the hands of time. Selling the Fountain of Youth puts billions of bucks in company coffers. Yet, the people I've interviewed are bucking this cultural current and have been telling a different story.

For example, women have said menopause is not what they feared. It marks the end of procreation, but it can also open opportunities to develop creative potential. The women in this study have talked about connecting with a deeper dimension of femininity, a greater sense of confidence in their womanly character and competence. Women in their fifties and sixties have also said that they are finding ways to recover a deeper, softer, more nurturing and attractive feminine side that was suppressed as they pursued second age success.

As they discover a new aspect of femininity, every one of them has said, "I still take great pride in my appearance." Some have also told me, "With greater freedom I am learning to appreciate being a woman more than ever." One man nearing sixty pointed to a picture of a radiant eighty-year-old woman, whose beaming face was lined with character. "I want to be like that when I grow up," he said. "That is true beauty, so much more real than the skin-deep prettiness of media models." The new woman has an attraction not based on mimicry of youth. She has a richer understanding of herself as a mature woman reflected in an appearance money cannot buy. For a woman to shift her perspective on what constitutes "true beauty," however, can be tough sledding. One striking fifty-something woman commented soberly, "Now, when I walk into a room with my twenty-five-year-old daughter, she's the one who turns the heads of the men. I used to get those double takes and the attention that followed. Those kinds of experiences remind me that I'm not the looker I once was. That's hard to swallow."

Similarly, men have also found ways to break the narrow, macho definition of "true manhood." Michael Gurian has suggested that one of the major issues men face growing up is to discover and define true maleness. In early manhood we need to prove ourselves and fill positions of responsibility and control. In growing up, men are on a quest to emulate traditional male models of hero, warrior, and patriarch. But the character of maleness changes as we mature. The psychiatrist Allan Chinen has discovered that as we grow older, the nature of the quest changes—or at least should change.

In midlife, men need to shed youthful models to release the powerful energy of deep masculinity that includes a repressed feminine side. Heroes and patriarchs can transcend competition and domination to become mentors, caregivers, and partners. Many of the men I've interviewed have told me that as they've matured they have been getting in touch with a feminine, more emotional side of their personalities, integrating these qualities into a fuller, mature masculinity. That combination makes biological as well as psychological sense. After all, men are only half-male. We men all started out female. It was the Y chromosome added to the X chromosome that shaped our maleness. Acknowledging the X side of us might be a natural way to experience integration after fifty. Affirming the X side of us and increasing our emotional intelligence don't diminish masculinity; they enrich it, as we tap creative potential and grow to become a whole person.

Redefining gender to fit a growing ideal self is important not only for an enhanced self-image but also to build and sustain intimate relationships. The new man is also more attractive, but not in the way defined by the gerontophobic media. Researchers and ordinary people are finding that love, attractiveness, and sex remain vital elements in happy marriages and intimate partnerships throughout a long third age. According to the usual view of aging, older people lose interest in sex and romance. Homes for the elderly used to split married couples into sex-segregated units. Thank heavens, another myth broken. I'll never forget ending an interview with a vibrant seventy-six-year-old woman who asked, "Why haven't you asked about sex? It's still so important." Recent studies of men and women in their sixties and seventies confirm her assertion. Many men have told me, "Our marriage has never been better. I'm discovering depths in myself, my wife, and our relationship I never imagined before."

The third age does not mark the end of sex and romance. On the contrary, expanded freedom allows couples to spend more time enjoying love and intimacy than they could find during a second age pursuit of external success. Not to mention liberation from having to disengage to cope with a wailing four-year-old who has just upchucked supper at eleven in the evening. As a seventy-five-year-old man once told me, "I'm no Don Juan, but my wife and I sometimes surprise ourselves by how we get it on after fifty years of marriage." Sex in the age of potency pills has added a new chapter about gender in many personal lives. For many of us, making love past sixty continues to be a peak experience in which our soul sings—and sings. We will see how other people are redefining gender in later chapters.

REDEFINING AND BALANCING WORK AND PLAY

One of the big surprises during my research was to discover a changing attitude towards work in people over fifty, a stance contrary to what I had expected. Thinking I would hear from these people that they were looking forward to the end of work in retirement, I was startled to hear them say, "Yes, my attitude towards work is changing. Work is becoming *more* important for me, not less." However, this positive affirmation was related to a changed understanding of the meaning of their work. In *The Third Age* few had even thought about retiring.

In recent research we have found many people in retirement who have also told us how important work remains for them in this period of their lives. Sometimes it's one of the most important interests. When that occurs, however, it changes the meaning of retirement. After leading me on a tour of her home filled with beautiful paintings she had created over the past twenty years, a seventy-six-year-old woman shared her story.

> After my children were old enough to attend school, I
> went to work in my husband's company and rose to
> become a merchandising manager and the number one
> buyer. This was quite an accomplishment for me, because
> I had no background in the field. I worked hard for twenty
> years and was proud of what I achieved. But when I was
> fifty-eight I told my husband it was time to make a
> change. When my children were very small I had taken
> courses in art school and discovered some talent. I was
> ready to develop that talent. I went back to art school and
> started painting. This is a whole new career. It's my pas-
> sion. I can't imagine not doing this work. If I don't, I get
> depressed. I see now that this is the work I was meant to
> do. It's who I am.

This woman retired from her job in order to invest her passion in creative work. Her passion also went into play. Painting was play as well as work; in addition she took up tennis and has become part of a prize-winning women's tennis team. More work and more play have filled the last eighteen years. Although some people might classify her as retired, this artist does not believe the word applies to her at all. Her eighty-four-year-old husband feels the same way. They don't find the term appropriate for this period in their lives. "We don't use the **R** word in this house," she told me.

In our research we have found many people whose lives defy a retired classification. These people include a semiretired architect who now focuses on his primary concern for urban and environmental restoration; a retired family therapist who has become a writer, teacher, and leader of reconciliation workshops; a decorator who has become a recognized leader in vital aging and environmental causes; a retired executive who devotes herself to helping nonprofit institutions; a retired school teacher who has become an artist and volunteer worker; a banker who has been a leader in nonprofit businesses; a retired social worker who has been developing new careers in theater and education; and a retired financial executive who left Boston and with his wife and has been designing a values-laden life in a small Maine community.

The people we have followed have been rediscovering how reframing work and play contributes to optimal development. In doing so, the boundaries between their work and their play become blurred. By sustaining this paradox they have put more flow into their lives.

Marty, a public school teacher who suffered burnout in his midfifties, surprised me with his story of how he overcame it. During a time when he felt his life was covered in sand, he also realized he had creative potential that had been buried by his job. He decided to try out new forms of work. In doing so, he made the important discovery "that my work is not my job." His job was what he had to do to earn a living and build his pension fund. His work, he said, was what he was working on: developing his skills as an artist. This activity was also his main form of play.

When he retired from his job at sixty, he had more freedom to follow his passion to do his real work. He concentrated on a variety of art forms: computer graphics, stained glass, painting, and carving. That is what he was doing when I was finishing the last book. In a follow-up I discovered that at sixty-five he decided he could apply his talents in a new way and signed up for two years in the Peace Corps in Africa. After returning home, he and his wife decided to relocate, selling their home in New York and moving to Florida. At seventy-three he still produces art works for fun as well as for profit, and he volunteers his expertise in building projects for indigent people. Instead of being an activity he had to perform, work has become part of the core definition of who he is becoming. "I'm still searching for the ultimate me," he once told me.

Marty's discovery that his work differed from his job can apply to most of us. We have grown up with an idea about work that was hatched during the Industrial Revolution. Work became a job that people usually perform away from home for money. But jobs are too narrow to hold a life. Even those of us who have chosen a professional career can find, after doing it for many years, that a once challenging form of work can turn into a deadening job. Our *real* work is different from a job. It's one major way we create and express ourselves. It gives shape and meaning to our lives. Work represents a contribution to the world, a way of adding value that has our signature on it. Work and parenting (a challenging form of work) are two primary ways of contributing a distinctive something that can benefit humanity and add joy to our lives. Most jobs don't seem to provide this opportunity. At its best, work represents a conversation with the world. Retirement, seen as not-working, kills the conversation. As we become older, many of us want an opportunity to change what we do as work, to make it something deeply personal, to shape it so that it expresses who we are becoming and provides us with meaning and enjoyment. Leaving a job can free us to find our real work. We are just starting to break free from an artificial notion of work derived from the Industrial Revolution and from a stunted notion of retirement that followed from it. Today we want to shape work that fits who we are becoming and how we want to live. The British business writer Charles Handy has written, "For the first time in human experience, we have a chance to shape our work to suit the way we want to live instead of always living to fit in with our work... We would be mad to miss the chance."

This opportunity is particularly appropriate for those of us in the third age. Most of us, having tried a number of jobs and careers, are ready to rediscover our passion and let it infuse those activities that are especially meaningful.

In words that reflect what so many people have told me during the past twenty years, Judy, a lawyer and former real estate entrepreneur, said of her work in the third age,

> I see myself as on a quest. It's both spiritual and physical. A major change in my life has to do with work. I have achieved a lot of worldly goals. Now I see my quest in these terms: how do I take my talents and experiences and put them to work in a larger sphere? Right now I'm asking about the meaning of life. Why are we here? What

should I be doing? I want to do something worthwhile. I've been discovering important areas in my life that are getting stronger. I appreciate my independence more, but I'm also defining more clearly what I have to offer people. Now I want to perceive my work as doing something for others, not just serving myself.

Searching for meaning, finding a way to express passion, and creating a broader sense of self can suffuse your third age redefinition of work. Here are questions that can help you redefine work and play.

- How do you define your work/career now?

- How does your redefinition of work fit with your own understanding of who you want to become? How do you express your passion?

- How will your third age work contribute to the legacy you want to leave?

- How do you define play now? How does it contribute to your evolving sense of self?

- How are you integrating play and work?

- How will your redefinitions of work and play influence the way you design and live your retirement?

Creating a Third Age Life Portfolio

Your third age journey is to become the person you can be. The creative balance of play and work builds a key passage to your identity. As the woman artist put it, "It's who I am." A major task is to shape your endeavors so that they enrich your journey through the third age. One way you can do this is to build a *third age life portfolio* that contains different kinds of work, careers, and play. But it will include much more. Similar to artists putting together portfolios, each of us will concentrate on different aspects of work, play, relationships, contributions, and self-care. At different times, each of us will hone skills in new areas, experiment with new activities, enlarge the scope of meaningful activities, become more involved with others, and retreat to have more time alone. A life portfolio opens up worlds and puts lives in balance.

A good time to build a third age life portfolio is before you start your transition into retirement. As one retiring business leader put it, "This process implies a change moving from one condition to another in a positive direction." It becomes, as he learned *a work in progress*. It keeps changing. If you haven't designed your portfolio yet, it's not too late to start. An emerging portfolio life can express both your pre-retirement planning and a redefinition of retirement. This process will add an important dimension of creativity to your life. It gives you a chance to become, as one woman put it, a *life artist*. Your world will become more complex, filled with activities, interests, commitments, and relationships that run in many directions at the same time. We shall have much more to say about this idea in chapter 7.

Sometimes people discover that in developing a portfolio life they embark on a third age career more fulfilling than an earlier one. One of our third age heroes has been former President Jimmy Carter, who has contributed so much to the world after he left the White House. He has set a precedent by using the American presidency as a stepping-stone to significant new careers. After leaving the White House, he was bitter about losing the election, in part because he felt he had been pushed out of his presidential career before he had

finished with it. Gradually he realized, helped by soulful conversations with his wife, how much more meaningful life
could be with greater freedom to devote himself to worthy
causes.

Leaving a premier executive position enabled him to tap
his potential and blossom in ways he hadn't dreamed of.
During his third age he has been engaged in rebuilding indigent communities, brokering peace between warring nations,
helping developing countries establish democratic process-
es, keeping up with the changing world and writing books,
providing civil leadership for the improvement of society, and
providing religious leadership in his faith community. The
value of his many contributions is recognized around the
world; winning the Nobel Peace Prize has been a fitting tribute. As he has reshaped a life of meaningful work, he has also
allowed more time for play, especially with his wife and family. Without using the term, he has actually been acting as a
pioneer in crafting a third age life portfolio.

A portfolio life, enriched by passion and creativity, conceived as a new form of leadership directed towards making
a difference to this world, can become your passage to a new
identity that greatly exceeds whatever you thought of yourself
in the second age.

BUILDING A MORE CARING LIFE

In the process of reinventing your identity, you are inevitably
led to question: what do I really care about? The great psychologist of the life cycle, Erik Erikson, claimed that a major
task in midlife is to acquire the virtue of *generativity*, caring for
the generations that follow. The term has been expanded to
mean caring for other people. In his large and penetrating

study of three different populations of men and women living into their eighties, George Vaillant discovered that those who age well care deeply for others. In his view, their caring is directly related to the quality of their lives. If you want to age well, open up and let the world in.

Most of those I've followed have been experiencing much warmer, caring, intimate relationships with spouses, partners, and family members. Another of the paradoxical principles is the expansion of freedom balanced with greater intimacy. I saw this most clearly in the married couples I observed. Often I've heard something like this: "My wife and I give each other freedom and support each other's growth. We keep rediscovering each other, which brings us closer together." When both partners grow, they find themselves in relationship to a beloved person who is changing positively, discovering and expressing new interests, traits, and qualities. Their mutual growth supports freedom and brings freshness to a relationship that could have become stale.

But greater interdependence and closeness also expose vulnerability. One man expressed what I've heard often: "I'm excited about the changes I'm experiencing. But one thing scares me. I don't know what I'd do if I lost my wife. We have become so close after thirty years of marriage. She is my best friend, my lover, my companion, and the center of our family. We have a wonderful marriage. I can't imagine living without her."

An intimate relationship that keeps getting better is another unexpected bonus of a fulfilling third age. As it warms our heart, it can also leave us breathless, as we become aware of life's mysterious goodness and fragility. As a sage once observed, life is measured not by the number of breaths we take, but by the moments that take our breath away. Often those moments come when we're with those we love.

Sometimes people outgrow a relationship. Several women and men found themselves suffocating in sterile marriages; they left home to build new lives. A few people in the study never married. Where there has been a loss or absence of one intimate partnership, I have seen growth stunted. But I have also seen people both with and without a marriage expand intimacy and caring in a widening circle of friends. Love in many of its forms plays more, not less of a role in our maturing lives.

Another paradox in mature development, especially as we enter retirement, is that the increase in personal freedom enables us to become more committed and more closely linked to others. Many people in the study report not only closer relationships with spouses, partners, and friends, but also with adult children, grandchildren, siblings, and extended family. They often become primary caregivers in families that are becoming intergenerational. Building more intimate, caring relationships while we are enlarging our freedom is a fundamental principle in third age growth. Retirement viewed as a period of liberation provides a wonderful framework for putting this principle into practice.

Like Jimmy Carter, the people in this study who have been investing in caring for their families have also been extending caring into organizations and communities. In later chapters we shall see how they have been making contributions to society in a variety of ways. Some have shaped their work so that it adds special value to projects or causes, such as environmental preservation, education, community relations, nonprofit organizations, and urban renewal. Giving has a more prominent role in an emerging third age identity. On her seventieth birthday the poet Maya Angelou was asked what she thought of growing older. "It's exciting," she said. And then she added:

I've learned that life sometimes gives you a second chance. I've learned that you shouldn't go through life with a catcher's mitt on both hands. You need to be able to throw something back. I've learned that whenever I decide something with an open heart, I usually make the right decision. I've learned that even when I have pains, I don't have to be one. I've learned that every day you should reach out and touch someone. People love a warm hug, or just a friendly pat on the back. I've learned that people will forget what you said, and forget what you did, but people will never forget how you made them feel.

What makes becoming older exciting is a growth process whereby our hearts open up and we touch more lives. In developing more caring personal identities, many have also become *keepers of meaning*, helping to shape institutions and the culture of the next generation. A friend of mine calls this kind of growth *becoming wisdom leaders*. Once we open the floodgates of caring, our lives will revitalize the world. We have been hearing from people that their caring often acquires a spiritual dimension. I have regularly asked people if they have become more or less religious. Few have said, more, a few have said, less, and some have said, never. But nearly all say they are becoming more spiritual, though sometimes that is admitted hesitantly. It depends on what we mean by *spiritual*.

The spirituality these people talk about is not necessarily or even primarily associated with religion. It is much more individual, often related to a growing sense of a caring connection with others, nature, and the cosmos. In addition to poetry and the arts, for some of us science has become a source of inspiration as it opens to us mysteries of a vast universe and billions of years of uninterrupted life. In moments of deep appreciation and wonder, we are silenced with awe before mystery, but we're also provoked. How can we express gratitude for all that has sustained our lives?

We can learn to become more open to the natural world and practice caring for creation that connects us to the immensity of the earth process. In writing about humans' role in the creation process, Thomas Berry suggests:

> We are venturing into a truly new type of experience. It requires a great deal of us. We did not choose to be here; the creation story selected us to be here. Once we are here, we must be willing to fulfill the destiny assigned to us; that is our grandeur, that is our blessedness, that is our joy, that is our peace. That is our gift to the great sacred community of existence. We are not making the journey alone, but with the entire universe community. Each of us, in our separate ways, is destined to be a significant personality in celebrating the past, grieving over the disasters of the present, and giving birth to the future.

As we grow older, our identities are enriched when we become aware that we are meaningfully linked to an evolutionary process that extends for billions of years. In building a more caring life, we are giving back to the process that has produced us. Time after time the people in the study have recounted how they have added dimensions to their lives by caring for others, for community, for earth, and for the future. A couple concerned about today's children has built a summer program for young leaders to help them design their lives using core values. A landscape architect has reinvented his work in semiretirement to contribute to urban renewal and environmental restoration. A retired oil executive, who once thought retirement would mainly consist of uninterrupted time to fish and play tennis, could not resist the opportunity to help his community by becoming a county commissioner.

Over and over I found people in the third age searching for ways to make a difference, to express genuine concern for those in need, for the future of our society and earth, for the wellbeing of children in generations to come. They are not retiring—they're advancing themselves and those whose lives they touch. Their caring nurtures a mature spirituality.

LEARNING SELF-CARE

In our unfolding lives we must also learn to balance altruistic caring for others with taking better care of ourselves. In the earlier part of this research I found that many people were having trouble with this challenge. Since then, the public message about the importance of self-care has connected with third agers. In the past ten years scientific research into successful aging has shown specifically how we can take better care of ourselves to extend our lifespan and improve the quality of our years. The Notes at the end of this book includes helpful references to consult. But self-care is still an issue that needs attention. Fully conscious caring for yourself smacks of narcissism. We have to learn to distinguish between healthy and unhealthy self-centeredness, another of the six paradoxical principles.

In *The Third Age* I wrote about one man who illustrated both the difficulty and the possibility of developing a broad based, healthy self-care. Fifty when I met him fifteen years ago, he was struggling with a serious flaw. An Episcopal priest who was in many respects an exemplary caregiver, the most difficult thing he has ever done, he said, was to announce to his congregation, "I am an alcoholic, and I need help." He entered a rehabilitation center where he sobered up and acquired the discipline needed to develop a different, healthy lifestyle. During that time, he kept hearing an inner voice, "You have to take care of yourself." But what did that mean? How was he to do that? He found self-care so difficult, because we do not have the philosophy or the language to express this idea adequately. It seems selfish.

In his fifties he became inventive, courageous, and committed to build a healthy lifestyle. He exemplified a balance we all need: to care for self and for others. His self-care included sobriety, exercise, good nutrition, and a balanced lifestyle with time for reflection, daily walks with his wife, and reading. He also devoted time to develop his musical talent, playing the guitar and singing. Five years after making a commitment to change, his life seemed to flourish.

You have to care about your own wellbeing as though it is a sacred trust. I discovered a text that suggests how self-care can have a spiritual dimension. In the apocryphal Gospel of Thomas, Jesus says:

> When you bring forth that which is within you, then that which is within you will save you.

> If you do not bring forth that which is within you, then that which is within you will destroy you.

That which is within you is your inner truth, the self that you can become. In his addiction the former priest was suppressing the best part of himself, and it was destroying him. If you don't care for your health, wellbeing, and growth, aren't you undermining your foundation for a fulfilling and purposeful life? In building a life that matters, you need to learn self-care, to bring forth the best that is within you. Care for yourself so that you can better care for others.

SO, WHAT'S NEXT?

THE LIVES OF THE PIONEERS ON THE THIRD AGE FRONTIER reflect options for sustained growth after fifty. The six principles of growth and renewal have produced in their lives a transformation of aging, new definitions of retirement, and a chance for profound happiness. Their stories should not inspire you to hold your course but to change it. Conventional wisdom has said that upon passing fifty you should live with your throttles depressed, start slowing down, and prepare to land. Second growth represents an alternative to inherited notions of retirement and aging. You have the capacity to shape your destiny and influence your future. Put the pedal to the metal, speed up, and get ready to take off. Three, two, one—liftoff.

Most people live fully for only a short time and extend the dying process way too long. With the advent of a third age, you need not go that route. The six principles offer an alternative of second growth for a long time after fifty. So live with throttles wide open. It's time to take off again and fly. To do so, you will have to shed old assumptions, expand your limits, think creatively, and live differently. You cannot rely on past accomplishments. Invention is called for. The way forward is dimly seen. The opportunity has only just knocked. You have so much more life in front of you. You can make of it what you want. Right now you have the invitation of a lifetime to change course for new growth. A few pioneers have shown all of us the way. The voyage is yours to take.

PART TWO

POSSIBILITIES
AND
LESSONS

CHAPTER FOUR

GRADUATION

And now the sun had stretched out all the hills,
And now was dropped into the western bay;
At last he rose, and twitched his mantle blue:
Tomorrow to fresh woods, and pastures new.

—MILTON, *Lycidas*

Vic: *I came to the idea of graduation because I didn't like the word* retirement.

At a third age retreat for retired corporate leaders who wanted to explore how the six principles of growth and renewal could help them redirect their lives, about a dozen men and women sat in a circle, introducing themselves. They summed up fascinating, wide-ranging careers and talked about plans for the future. As we were completing the circle, Vic, who had been a manufacturing executive vice president for a global producer of commercial equipment, began his introduction with an arresting comment: "When I left the company after thirty years, I didn't retire. I graduated, and that meant a commencement of something new and different."

In a moment of quiet suspense, both participants and facilitators started to take in the implication of this powerful metaphor that reframes the entire experience of retirement. The leaders gathered in that circle had said that they were trying to see retirement as an opportunity—a release from the stresses and pressures of corporate responsibility and a chance to design and live more fulfilling personal lives. Work had brought them professional satisfaction and many rewards, but success in careers had costs that they had begun to identify as they struggled with their own personalized definition of retirement. By the end of the five-day retreat, most of the other participants had adopted Vic's metaphor. Vic's reframing of the event with a fresh term had breathed new life into their own planning for retirement, a process that each had so far experienced with varying degrees of ambivalence.

The quality of your life depends so much on how you choose to perceive it. If you see your journey after retirement as a descent from a career peak, as some sort of diminishment, you're likely to experience decline in various aspects of your life. "Over the hill," right? Many people see themselves this way but are afraid to admit it. We all know such people and have likely wondered about their deterioration, and perhaps worried about falling into a similar bog. Retirement can become a gradual hibernation, as people feel they have been marginalized, relegated to roles as life's second stringers or spectators. Many people simply check out. Retirement—graduation rather—could instead become a grand entrance, an esplanade to new *life peaks*.

Graduation means to pass from one stage to another, usually a higher one. To perceive your life as rising to a higher level of meaning and satisfaction, you need a compelling, positive image to shape a desirable scenario. Vic's image not only changed how he saw life after retirement but also enabled him to redesign the course he would take. Retreat participants agreed that it makes a lot of sense to reframe retirement as a graduation, especially when a person feels vibrant and healthy, possessing a reservoir of untapped potential, and expecting many more years to apply it. His metaphor helped others in the retreat see more clearly the future as a commencement, as a change in course providing fresh opportunities and exciting challenges—not to go over the hill, but rather to climb another mountain.

At the end of the retreat, one leader, Lou, observed that this experience had both unsettled him and inspired him. A former senior executive with a worldwide energy company, for two years Lou had been content with the repose of a retirement that had afforded him unlimited free time to enjoy himself, particularly to fish and play tennis. All play and no work was what he had thought he wanted. But in reflecting about the meaning of his life in the near future, Lou discovered two important areas needing attention: his marriage and his work, which he had until then relegated to the past.

The following year Lou returned with his wife for another retreat to continue planning *their* commencement. He also reported that in addition to pursuing his twin passions of fishing and tennis, he had responded to a local community need by volunteering to serve as a county commissioner. Work, redefined outside the corporate setting, was becoming a new and vital part of his retired life. Lou was learning to think about retirement as commencement into a more complex life than he had imagined when for the last time he turned out the lights and closed the door to his office in the executive suite.

The authors were intrigued by Vic's idea of graduation. In reading and in interviews we had not seen that particular term used before. After the retreat we interviewed Vic several times to learn more about his choice of metaphor, how it had helped him redirect his life, and how it might help us all rethink and redefine retirement.

> I came to the idea of graduation as a term to describe what I was doing (leaving work for pay), because I didn't like the word *retirement*. I had an image of pulling up the drawbridge and filling the moat with alligators. What appealed to me about graduation, a term I hadn't seen used before, was that it implied a change of state, moving from one position to another in a positive direction. Graduation has allowed me to learn more about myself; I don't think of myself as introspective. It also encourages me to get into activities that I had neither the time nor interest for as an undergraduate.

For many people retirement primarily signifies an ending rather than a beginning. "I've paid my dues. It's time to ease up and do nothing," is what we've typically heard from retirees. At fifty-nine Vic knew that he and his wife of nearly forty years had much more life to live, and they did not want to spend it the prescriptive ways pre-retirement programs typically suggest. They decided to graduate together. By leaving the company they were concluding one successful course in life to start another. Initiating this change challenged them in several ways. Until Vic approached retirement he had not been particularly introspective. Preparing for graduation prompted him to become more reflective and to learn more about himself. This quality of mind became a new dimension of his personality. In our conversations with him he always talks about new learning.

The metaphor of graduation does more than give retirement a facelift. It provides an invigorating viewpoint for building a new sense of personal identity, a foundation for sustained growth. Vic sees himself as a graduate rather than as a person who has retired, someone who is beginning something rather than someone who has ended something. The latter prospect by and large reflects a diminished self-image. Retiring often suggests a retreat to the sidelines, being shunted off to a restricted space. To Vic retirement smacked of incarceration, like being locked in a castle with no way out, drawbridge up, the moat filled with alligators. How can you aspire to a new version of success with that dismal scenario?

The psychiatrist Allan Chinen believes that a major challenge for men in midlife is to create a new self-image. During second age men often seek to fill the roles of hero, warrior, and patriarch, a drive to be successful in the competition for desired achievement and positions of control. During third age men should outgrow these winning-is-everything roles and develop new, deeper ones, more appropriate to our age.

Vic had been both hero and patriarch. Seeing retirement as graduation enabled him to put aside dominant second age roles and tap unrecognized masculine depths. As we pointed out in chapter 3, building a positive third age identity allows us to achieve greater integration of masculine and feminine, intellect and intuition, practical competence and creativity. As we'll see, Vic integrated his feminine values with his masculine side to become a supportive caregiver. In the modern idolatry of second age achievement, many men seem to have lost an appreciation of a deeper dimension in selfhood and masculinity. Reframing retirement as a graduation can free us from the compulsion for external success to become a more complete self. Vic's metaphor enabled him to see life after paid employment as teeming with opportunities. It has provided him with an empowering self-image as a mature, masculine graduate commencing a journey to a different kind of leadership and greater satisfaction and fulfillment.

Vic's mindful reflection has led him to realize, as it does for many graduates, that tapping his potential requires him to risk significant changes. His new identity leads him to search, explore, question, and experiment. One of the first decisions he and his wife made was to pull up stakes to make a new home in what they would define as an ideal location. They explored several parts of the country and chose northern California because it fit so well with their expanding interests in spending more time outdoors for the whole year.

Like new graduates everywhere, they began a new life. This transition proved to be more challenging than they had thought it would be, but "we would do it all over again." It took more time than expected to get established in the new community and to make new friends. Since their family was now scattered around the country, this location required more complicated arrangements for reconnecting. But the benefits of the new community far outweighed the complications. This relocation was, he told us, the first time he and his wife had been able to choose where to live. The company had previously made those decisions for them.

After making the move, Vic was unexpectedly called upon to play a new role as a caregiver to his father, who was dying of cancer at his home in Florida. Vic spent a huge amount of time with his father over the next two years; this commitment required much flying back and forth. The visits with his father were demanding, but also rewarding. Vic reported, "I got to know him much better than I ever did during some sixty years. And I really liked him." Being with his dad in his final days was both important and meaningful. Vic's caregiver role soon expanded unexpectedly, when his wife's heart stopped beating for five to ten seconds, causing her to fall and crack her skull. The fall caused a concussion. An independent and strong willed person, she didn't take kindly to having a caregiver husband. But their strong marriage only got stronger during her eventual complete recovery. They celebrated her recovery by planning a special celebration of their fortieth wedding anniversary.

In reflecting on what this new role had meant, he wrote, "Two very important relationships were strengthened through care giving, which has been a tremendous learning experience for me that will be useful in the future." By defining this phase in life as a commencement to unexpected, unplanned experiences, Vic felt freer to take on this new care-giving role with determination and dedication. As he was developing a more nurturing masculinity, he was learning to make a different kind of contribution outside the corporate world.

Vic's commencement plan had a new focus, which was to take better care of himself. He regularly spends time outdoors, biking and hiking near his home. He's also developing his mind through increased levels of reading. Currently, his interest is in history. Both he and his wife are excited about learning more about other cultures and parts of the world. They have begun carefully planned travel expeditions, often with other members of their family. Travel, he reported, has become a big part of their third age life portfolio, providing fun, learning, and new challenges that they didn't have time for before graduation. Recently they discovered an association called Friendship Force, people interested in traveling to other countries and staying in homes of people who will in return stay with them in this country. "This may turn out to be a major source of enjoyment and cultural learning," he wrote us.

Like others in our study, Vic has reflected on and rethought the meaning of work for the third age. In our early conversations with him he didn't like to think about work, a term still tied up with his involvement with the corporation he had left behind. Like many people, he had equated work with a job, and he had put his job well behind him. Retirement had come to mean not-working. Two diametrically opposed worlds, *working* and *not-working*, and, like the *Star Trek* episode that explores competing universes: if they would ever meet, the world would explode, or implode, or both.

But to Vic graduation suggests moving ahead to new perspectives and experiences. Gradually he learned that he could reframe work to signify several meaningful endeavors, which he was free to pursue on a volunteer basis. Not only can working and not-working meet without cosmological catastrophe, their fusion creates new opportunities. With an adequate pension, he could put *working for pay* behind him, but he engages in other forms of work that enable him to contribute to society. Vic became active in Kiwanis in his adopted city and accepted the role of Kiwanis Advisor to a high school Key Club. In this role he has become a mentor and friend to teenagers, who have invited him to join their projects; he's also become a chaperone when they travel. Although both a father and grandfather, he had never had an experience like this. This different kind of work provides him with a new way of mentoring, both satisfying and fun.

Vic has also become involved in SCORE, the Service Corps of Retired Executives. Members offer free services to entrepreneurs who want to go into business for themselves or who want to expand a business. Vic finds this business coaching particularly rewarding, being both work and learning at the same time. While he has engaged in other volunteer activities, at this point most of his work is done here. Through it he has learned that if he had had the chance, his career would have been as an "individual contributor or small business person rather than a corporate type." His new work has become a journey of self-discovery and self-redefinition. His graduation has given him the opportunity to realize a dream by helping others advance in an arena he passed by. Commencement has opened a side of his personality that had been suppressed in a thirty-year career with a major corporation. He later released his entrepreneurial side by jumping into a new enterprise as a founder and senior board member.

In the five years following his graduation, Vic has been putting together a third age life portfolio, a task he says that will last a lifetime. As a follow-up to several conversations, he wrote us that it feels like he's painting on an empty canvass. It doesn't pay to worry about filling it up; he's content to see his new life as "a work in progress." Graduating has given him the freedom and flexibility to keep adding new sketches to the canvass. As we review his progress, his growth is leveraged by the six principles of growth and renewal recapped in chapter 3. At the core of his commencement enterprise is the formation of a fuller, deeper, more mature identity. By redefining retirement, he has been changing course to create a rich and fulfilling third age.

Ed: *I learned that I should think about retiring to rather than retiring from.*

The story of Ed's creative growth and renewal during his fifties was in *The Third Age*. A university tennis coach and physical education professor in an East Coast university, at fifty Ed took a sabbatical that changed his life. Until then, his focus, quite natural for his career, had been on winning in competitive environments. On sabbatical in an outdoors program with youngsters, he discovered a side of his personality that was surprisingly new to him. He felt a powerful sense of compassion. This value led him to transform his entire life. Ed began to redefine work and play by infusing them with interpersonal values.

During the next seven years he totally changed the way he related to members of his teams: he became a warm, supportive, friendly coach who built teamwork and camaraderie among the players and himself. Ironically, the players performed as well if not better than ever. In his late fifties he retired as coach and became the department chair of physical education. He also kept his commitment to work with youngsters by developing new outdoors programs for them. Ed's life was paradoxically becoming both more focused and more expanded in several important areas: career, community, family, close friendships, a hobby of bee raising, and regular exercise in sports and the natural environment. In the early part of his third age he exemplified the six principles of growth and renewal.

In his early sixties Ed realized that he was nearing retirement and should start preparing for it. He attended a preretirement planning workshop, at which he learned that he should think about *retiring to* rather than *retiring from*. That idea led him to once again revise his unfolding life. Without actually using the term, he began preparing for a graduation that would send him in a different but positive direction. When he finally graduated at sixty-five, he had a well-thought-out ten-year plan for an active lifestyle with clearly defined areas and lots of flexibility. With his commencement underway, he said:

> I have a plan that will take me to when I'm seventy-five, when I will probably start winding down. For now I'm building a new business, spending lots more time with family and friends, traveling with my wife, staying active

in several sports and outdoor experiences, and community involvement. I like this life, especially the freedom. I
don't have the pressure of "have to" anymore. I miss the
university and friends there, but we stay in touch. I'm
excited about what's coming next.

Ed thought long and hard about where he wanted his life
to go. Some of his close friends had been retiring to the golf
course or to Florida in RVs. That lifestyle was not how he
imagined leveraging his new freedom. He instead visualized
the future as an opportunity to design an active life in which
he could finally devote himself fully to those activities and
relationships that matter most to him. One of these activities
was to plunge himself into a new form of work.

Ed had for years been developing a hobby raising bees, a
pastime that had been difficult to maintain as a coach,
because bee season runs from April into the summer, right
when university tennis competition is at its peak. Upon graduating from his university career, Ed threw himself into this
work. From April through July, beekeeping has become a fulltime career. He has also been building a network with others
and was elected president of his state beekeepers association. Under his leadership this organization has been reaching out to young people, introducing them to beekeeping. Ed
has expanded his operation to several farms, increasing production that has good prospects of modest revenues soon
and the potential for more later. To introduce the product
within the region, he and his wife travel to local festivals
where they sell honey products. His tasty honey is acquiring
name recognition. He's excited about this new line of work
that provides him with an ongoing challenge and enjoyment,
opportunities for meeting new people and travel, learning,
and a supplemental income.

In planning his journey, Ed designed his life around key priorities. One of these goals was to transform an enjoyable hobby into a rewarding, successful enterprise. Another priority is family. Ed and his wife have been married forty years. His life plan includes lots of free time, after a hectic beekeeping season, to be engaged with his wife, children, and first grandchild. Travel is a third priority. Their four adult children have given him and his wife a trip to Rome, where she has family she has not had the chance to meet. After their Italian trip, they have been making plans to travel around the United States touring National Parks. Now that he is not bound by a sense of *having to*, he and his wife are using their new freedom to take trips they've always dreamed about. They have always enjoyed camping; now they have time to camp in areas that have been out of reach because of a tight schedule.

In addition to work and travel Ed has spent more time with his sons and son-in-law. In redesigning his life, he has given significant space to playing. He has always seen himself as a "player." Graduation has given him the freedom to play with his sons and good friends outdoors in kayaking, canoeing, biking, hiking, and on the golf course. Outdoors activity is a fourth priority. It is where he plays. For him the outdoors issues constant invitations to work, play, be himself, and connect with those he loves and cares about. Because he has always spent so much time outdoors with young people, Ed still feels vital and youthful. Asked how old he feels, he replied, "I feel I'm about forty. I see seniors my age, and I just don't feel or act as they do. Time with youngsters, and with my sons, has kept me young." Taking care of himself is another priority. He's enjoying the second growth alternative to aging discussed in chapter 2. By focusing on the idea of *retiring to*, Ed has been creatively designing a third age life portfolio that opens up new possibilities for the rest of his third age.

Betty: I *don't think of this as retirement. I don't like the word. I see it as the next phase in my life, as part of an ongoing journey. It's a wonderful phase.*

Sitting in her lovely home redolent with fresh cuttings of spring flowers from her English garden, Betty reflected on her life and made this telling comment, "I feel very blessed. I'm so grateful to have a life congruent with my values." How has this sixty-two-year-old woman reached this enviable state? The answer lies in a combination of factors—determination, creativity, and good fortune, among others. More significant, she revealed herself to be another person who has been tapping her potential to design a full life and redefine retirement. Her story provides answers that are more practical than a list of important attributes.

As she finished college, Betty aspired to become a teacher and enrolled in a master's program in education at Stanford University. After receiving a degree she began teaching history in a local high school. She soon met and married Bob, who was studying to become a cardiologist. For the next few years they moved back and forth from the West Coast to the East Coast so that he could complete training, internship, and residency. At first she continued teaching, but she let that go when she had a baby boy. A couple of years later, as Bob was starting a practice, she had a girl. Eventually they moved into a lovely home next door to Stanford, where Bob has been a professor in the medical school for the past thirty years. As a young mother Betty concentrated on raising her children. As her children grew, she started developing creative talents. She took an art class, did a lot of painting, and applied her artistic skills to both the interior of her home and an expanding garden.

As the children grew up and went off to school, Betty volunteered in community projects. Detecting a high level of stress in her local community, she soon became an expert in stress management and offered stress management programs for the community, corporations, and the medical school. Recognizing her special talents, the Chamber of Commerce appointed her as a Director of Leadership, a position that she grew to love. She wasn't about to change it. Yet during this time her region was exploding with new enterprises in the field of technology.

Sensing her special capabilities and a local need, John Gardner, a paragon of American leadership, persuaded her to start up a leadership foundation for corporate executives in Silicon Valley. The aim was to help them expand their vision and activities to serve the common good. At forty-eight, with her son in college and her daughter finishing high school, she felt that she could devote herself fulltime to this original enterprise. She started the foundation by herself, with no money and no resources, only her commitment, talents, and the mentoring support of John Gardner. Through this experience they became close friends. Within a few years the foundation was flourishing, and her leadership of business executives was greatly appreciated and recognized.

Having guided this organization for nearly a dozen years and realizing that she would soon be sixty, Betty decided to take time off to catch her breath and reflect. She and her husband, who love to go on adventures together, this time went on an African safari. As often happens when we place ourselves in a foreign context, Betty started listening to an inner voice that had been suppressed by heavy responsibilities; she began to wonder if it was time to retire.

This job had been an exhilarating challenge and provided her with an exceptional opportunity to grow, meet wonderful people, and make a difference. The foundation was in excellent shape; she could turn over its leadership to others, while continuing to serve on its board. Twelve hard years were enough; while extremely rewarding, this job was consuming her life. For years she had been leaving home at seven in the morning and not returning until after seven in the evening. Programs regularly took her away for days at a time. While on safari Betty felt the need to reclaim a personal life, and she sensed that there were other adventures awaiting her.

Soon after returning from the trip she stepped down. Like many graduates who take time off before commencing a new life, for the next six months Betty did nothing. A wise counselor had told her to accept no offers until she was ready to move towards her newly clarified goals as guided by her values. *Don't just do something; sit there.* In thinking about retirement, Betty, like Vic, realized that she didn't like the term. It didn't convey what she had in mind, a new phase in a continuing journey of personal development. What she wanted was more freedom, more discretionary time to focus on those aspects of life that were most important, many of which had been given too little attention during her twelve years as a CEO of a nonprofit foundation. More freedom, more time for family and friends, more travel, more opportunity for learning and spiritual growth—that's where Betty was headed.

But life's journey doesn't follow a straight course. Within the next year she was to experience painful losses. Her mentor, John Gardner, contracted cancer. She spent many hours with him as he lay dying. Losing him hurt, but similar to the death of aging parents, his death was an expected loss. What she didn't expect was that her sister-in-law, who had become a best friend, died suddenly of a stroke in just one day. That loss shattered her. While planning the new phase in life, she had counted on having at least twenty-five years with her sister-in-law. They had dreamed of "growing outrageous together in our old age."

The losses sent her into a depression, a detour not part of her imagined itinerary. Betty decided that she needed help in coping with the grief; she found a grief counselor, who convinced her that there was no shortcut to healing.

> She was a wonderful grief counselor. I learned you have to do the grief work now or later. I decided to do it. That took a whole year—the toughest time is the first year, especially when you go through an anniversary or an event that had been so meaningful. I miss her so much. The grief work involved talking about her, sharing feelings with family and friends, learning it's okay to cry. That's part of the price of you pay for loving someone. I'd rather have that pain than not have had such a rich experience. As I worked through my grief, there were finally moments when I started to experience joy—like when you suddenly realize you're laughing again. I came out of this year realizing more than ever how precious life is. You need to appreciate the moment.

While completing her grief work, Betty was beginning to sense even more clearly core values and make other positive changes in her life. She prioritized her values, around which she was to design the next phase of her life. Time with the family came first. Betty and Bob have had a long, close marriage; they plan together for quality time. They both love the outdoors and have taken trips that allow them to be active while seeing new sights, like the safari and cycling trips to Europe. As she said about her safari experience, she wanted more new adventures in her life, especially with her family. Their son was recently married, and she looks forward to grandchildren. They are also pleased with their daughter, who chose to enter a graduate theology degree program. Betty identifies with her daughter's direction, because of her own spiritual awakening during her grief work.

Affirming the value of family, Betty has rediscovered the role of homemaker and now spends more time there. She has revived her decorating skills to make her English cottage home beautiful and welcoming. Gardening has also become more important and another way to express her talents. She spends a lot of time selecting plants, then planting and caring for them. She has a wide assortment of flowers that she uses to decorate the home. Several times a year she invites friends and neighbors over to enjoy their home, the flowers, and each other.

It's fun to share our home with friends. April is a fun time—we have special gatherings to share the garden with people. We pick flowers to share them with friends. One of the great joys of my life is being connected, bringing people together who would not otherwise come together. I love to create an environment where people feel safe to explore new ideas and relationships. This is a small kind of adventure, which is more possible now.

Another aspect in her third age life portfolio was a reassessment of the place of work in this next phase. After waiting six months, Betty considered working with a variety of nonprofit organizations that had missions congruent with her commitments and values. Work remained an adventure she wanted to keep open. In fact, the joy she referred to in home events closely resembled her own definition of her work as a leader:

Leadership is a creative process. I love to create programs, and to create an environment that allows people to be free and to grow. We did that in the leadership foundation. I love to bring people together where something happens that would not have otherwise. That's part of the challenge of being a leader. It gets your creative juices going. You feel so much more alive.

Betty's enthusiasm and extraordinary competence attracted many organizations that wanted her assistance. She tried hard to be selective. But within a couple of years she was consulting and serving on six boards, two of which required major amounts of time. Retiring was supposed to have brought more discretionary time. She began to wonder where that time had disappeared. When we last spoke with her, she had decided to cut back, to allow more time for other core values, and to consider another line of work. What's next? Something different, perhaps: "I had such outstanding grief counseling. It inspired me. Doing that or working in a hospice interests me a great deal. Grief counseling was a very spiritual experience. I haven't done anything like this before, but I am seriously considering getting training to enter this field. It fits with another part of my life, which is to develop spiritually."

Her spiritual interests arose several years earlier in an unusual context. During the last few years as an executive, Betty was having conversations with other leaders who introduced a topic not usually found in the business world. These leaders confessed that they sometimes experienced a spiritual dimension in their work. They were, ironically, having less to do with organized religion, but they felt themselves becoming more spiritual.

This topic of spirituality resonated with Betty. She has long been a member of a Congregational Church but attends formal services only occasionally. The grief work prompted an awakened spirituality. She also found her spirituality growing outdoors. She wanted to feel a personal relationship with God that didn't seem readily available in church. With another former executive and good friend she has recently begun a birding program. Each week they walk in the hills following birds.

This birding program is really a spiritual experience—to have a bird appear, learn about it, and have it part of my life. I'm feeling a connection with birds that is new. I first had the experience on safari—now it's something I'm devoted to. I often feel my spirit awakening outdoors. I love nature. This spiritual side of my life is important now. I've gone to seminars and learned a lot. I've been reading spiritual masters from different traditions. I've just finished a trip exploring a different spiritual tradition. My spirituality spreads through my life now—in my family, in making a contribution to the community, in creativity, and in nature. I often take a popular hike up a hill behind our house. On a clear day you can see the East Bay hills, and the hills between the ocean and us. It's just glorious. I might walk alone or with a friend. When I get to the top, I feel so blessed and say, "Thank you, God." This makes my soul sing.

Her own spiritual development has become another core value that has become an integral part of her journey.

Betty's definition of her journey has been striking a balance among different values: providing a service and having adventures, serving as a homemaker and a community leader, engaging in the politics of organizations, stepping aside to develop her own spirituality, refining seasoned skills, and experimenting with new ideas. Her schedule is still often jammed packed with multiple commitments. As a devoted caregiver, how does she find the time to take care of herself?

Oh, I'm taking better care of myself these days. We have a healthy diet, sleep enough, and exercise. After all, I'm married to a cardiologist! I try to exercise every day, but I cheat some. So it's not quite seven days. I walk a lot and try the hills. I drink less alcohol—but we drink better

wines. I'm too old to drink cheap wine. Actually one of
our hobbies is to collect good wine. I'm trying to stay in
shape to live a long, healthy life. I sense I have a long
time left—maybe I'll live into my nineties. I feel now is
prime time. So I have a philosophy now that says you
should do what you believe in, because you don't know
what might happen. Do it now while you have the chance.

Like others we've interviewed, Betty has been taking care
of herself while she increases the care she extends to others.
The energy of caring is not limited, like a set quantity. Caring
does not become a scarce resource through use. Rather it's
like a flame: the hotter it gets, the wider its radius. The more
we add to the fire, the bigger it gets. Building a more caring
life energizes us. The contributions she has been making
brighten the lives of many people. Recently, the leadership
foundation had a reunion, where it affirmed its mission and
thanked her for her leadership.

There were over a hundred and fifty people celebrating
our work. It was reassuring to see the continuity, the
ongoing commitment of all of us. It made me feel grateful
to have contributed to that. People keep saying what a
legacy we've left. I feel good about that legacy that is
enriching other people's lives. This process will continue.
I'm fortunate to be part of it.

As she commences in this new phase of her life, Betty has
been redefining success as she develops a life centered on
core values and leaves a legacy that is enriching many people
at home, in local organizations, and in the wider community.
Betty's life portfolio since her graduation has been shaping
the person she is becoming in her third age. As she looks
ahead, she believes she will redefine aging: "It should be full

of vitality and a time to make a contribution." At this point her life seems to be coming together in a satisfying whole.

El: *The first twenty-six years were for the company; the next twenty-six are for Stephanie and me. What has changed over the years is that I have found great satisfaction in community service, so I can give back while pursuing personal interests.*

Vic, Ed, and Betty have gotten off to a good start. They have creatively changed course and have long-term plans that should carry them far. How far? How might this journey look in ten or fifteen years? One person who left the corporate world to design an entirely different kind of life sixteen years ago provides an encouraging answer. El's story of remarkable growth and renewal during his fifties was told in *The Third Age*. The latest chapter in his story is even more remarkable.

When he was forty-eight and a senior financial officer of a Fortune 500 corporation, El walked into his boss's office to announce that he was retiring. That announcement was astonishing, for he had been perceived as an extremely able leader, a company man, and a likely candidate for the top position in finance. Little did people realize that El had another side to him beneath his three-piece suit. Like others in our study, El loved outdoor experiences—in particular hunting, fishing, and hiking through the woods. He and Stephanie, his former high school sweetheart and wife of twenty-five years, had been thinking about retirement for years. They both wanted freedom to develop a satisfying life away from corporate pressures, urban frenzy, the engulfing current of consumption, and "keeping up with the Joneses." They were beginning to listen to recurring dreams of fulfilling activities. A new development in El's life prompted a change in course. In his forties El had started a new hobby of wood-carving and became so good at it that he started winning prizes. Longing to have more time for his hobby, he sensed that his corporate career conflicted with his emerging creativity. His genius was looking for a way out of the bottle. Ironically, the company sent El to a wellness seminar for leaders, an experience that resulted in his gain, their loss. On the first day he was given the task of stating his purpose in life. He had never thought about this point. Excelling in conservative, fiscal management, he didn't ask about purpose. After an agonizing solitary morning, he emerged with his statement: "The purpose of my life is to become the person I can be, to realize my potential, and to share." This realization of an emerging core identity was to change his life.

Coming home from the seminar, he huddled with Stephanie to reach a decision to take retirement as soon as possible. On New Years Day they met with their three sons to talk over their dream and plans. Since two sons had finished college and the third was halfway through, they realized they had enough saved to support the third through college and to settle in a new place. A pension, investments, and a simpler life style would enable them to afford their dream. Within a year they had moved to a farm in northwestern Maine, where Stephanie opened an antique store and El set up a studio in which he could carve away to his heart's content.

A check-in seven years later revealed they were fulfilled and happy with their new life. Stephanie's antique business was flourishing. They had a dual career marriage, where he helped manage the store and sell his carvings. Their farm was producing a bumper crop of blueberries, adding the dimension of farmer to his workplan and personal identity. A flexible work schedule gave El the time he had always wanted to hunt and fish. He had perfected his fishing skill so much that he was giving talks about fly-fishing and had started a book on the subject. In addition to work and play, El applied his managerial skills to local town organizations and his church. Sharing, he said, was even more important to him then than it had been; he hadn't had an opportunity to share as a corporate executive. Both of them were involved in community affairs and had a growing network of good friends. He wrote, "It is a wonderful experience to go into town and know almost everyone you meet and be able to call most of them friends. Many people in this community have chosen to live here for reasons similar to ours. These shared values provide a strong basis for friendship."

Ten years after graduating El and Stephanie had an enviable life, having dared to make a long-shared dream come true. Leaving the company was a graduation with an impressive commencement. El was still amazed at what they had accomplished:

I am still awed by the realization when I wake up that the day is mine to structure. This is so different from my life in the corporation. We did exactly the right thing. The first twenty-six years after college were for the company; the next twenty-six are for Stephanie and me. We now have what we want. We enjoy each day. What's next? We plan to continue what we're doing.

In thinking about the change in course he had made, El was motivated to create a purposeful life. It was unusual for an experienced expert in financial planning to switch gears and become a dreamer. But while working for the company, he had carried in his daily planner a quote by Thoreau: "If one advances confidently in the direction of his dreams and endeavors to live the life which he has imagined, he will meet with success unexpected in common hours."

This right-brained message connected with his left-brain planning aptitude. Like Betty's safari experience, the wellness seminar prompted him to seize the day and advance towards his dreams. Discovering a sense of purpose led El to develop his capacity for mindful reflection and risk taking. He did not develop this growth principle alone. He and Stephanie had long, frequent, intimate discussions about what they wanted in life. They have continued to share thoughts and dreams in an ongoing dialogue. In their new setting they often began the day with a ninety-minute walk through the woods or down a road through their fields. This dialogue was to lead them to even more changes in their lives.

Reconnecting with him as he completed sixteen years in his new environment, we found sustained growth that has been amazing. "But how do you do it?" we asked. "How do you keep on growing?" His sharing of his story through conversations and e-mails has helped us understand how this process can be sustained. We've learned that his statement of purpose has been a guiding influence in his life, helping him define who he is and where he sees his life going. Creating a positive third age identity has been the core principle of his growth. He has kept his vision alive, remaining committed to become the person he can be, to realize his potential, and to share. Underlying his vision is a set of core values: "You probably have noticed, I am a traditionalist with conservative values. Yet at the same time I believe we should dream and imagine the life we want to live. I kid Stephanie that when my epitaph is written it will go something like this: 'He lived the life he was blessed with to the fullest.'"

El's vision and values have led him to redefine not merely retirement but also work and play, success, relationships with loved ones and the community, and his legacy. Though he sees himself as a traditionalist, the way he expresses his conservative values makes him positively avant-garde. He continues to be a leading pioneer on the third age frontier. In graduating, El had also started to design a third age life portfolio of activities that was to expand and become more complex. While he initially saw his new life allowing him to hunt, fish, carve, and spend more time with his wife and family, he gradually realized that community service was becoming a major new form of work. He combined personal interests with community needs, becoming involved in enterprises focused on regional development, conservation, young people, wildlife and fisheries, and historical preservation. Part of his new self-definition called for sharing. El surprised himself by how important this interest has become: "What has changed over the years is that I have found a great deal of satisfaction in community services that combine my interest in history and the outdoors, so that I can give back while pursuing personal interests. With my focus on planning for independence, I never could have anticipated some of the activities I am now involved with on a daily basis."

Local people have appreciated El's contributions through community service. As he turned sixty-four, he was roasted by the Historical Society, an organization he has led to become widely recognized in the state. Later the same year the Chamber of Commerce presented him and his wife with a community service award with special recognition for the leadership of Junior Guides and the Sportsman's Association, a local organization he helped make the largest and most effective in Maine. "My work now," he said, "is what I do while pursuing my interests." Having just completed a big, multiyear project on the governor's Advisory Council for Fisheries and Wildlife Restoration, he has created time to establish an Outdoor

Sporting Heritage Museum, another multiyear project including museum design, fund raising, construction, collection display, and administration. He has also committed to compiling a book on regional history. These enterprises alone will keep El occupied until he finishes his second twenty-six years.

Completion of the big project just mentioned represented another significant change. As he was nearing sixty, he and Stephanie discovered a hundred-year-old hunting and fishing lodge threatened with demolition in spite of its esteemed heritage. They hated to see it go, because it represented a lifestyle and set of values that had become dear to them. Stephanie was beginning to see an end to her career in the antique business, which she could conclude after giving it a dozen years.

With a lot of soul-searching dialogue they eventually achieved a vision of buying and restoring this lovely old lodge and making it into their home. They took a big risk and purchased the property, and El spent the next four years overseeing its restoration. Stephanie retired from her business so they could sell the farm and move into this charming setting on the edge of a beautiful lake ringed by forested mountains. Their home has become a center for expressing their core values—supporting family and community, conservation, educating the young, and sustaining a valued tradition for future generations. The restored lodge symbolizes values they want to instill in young people; it stands as a legacy they are leaving to this region.

When he left the company, El's original intention was to use the freedom to hunt, fish, carve, and spend quality time with his wife. Like Lou who had looked forward to fishing and playing tennis, El had thought that much of his commencement would be devoted to play. But during the years work has continued to share center stage, though the boundaries of work and play have remained fuzzy. He might have difficulty applying a single label to most of his activities. Although many activities had not been anticipated, they did not occur by accident; his endeavors are carefully planned. His outlook expresses an optimistic openness to discovery with a carefully worked out strategy for continued change. He explained his view of his life this way:

> I look for new challenges (the lodge) and opportunities (Junior Guides and Sportsman's Association), evaluate them, and select the ones that fit best with my goals, dreams, and who I am. I replace activities that no longer measure up (antique business) with the new. It's like a funnel, where I constantly search out new projects, analyze them, and filter out the ones that are important enough to devote necessary time and energy. The new projects keep the old ones a little fresher.
>
> Another thing that keeps my journey going forward is to concentrate on those things I do better than I used to— enjoy other people, share my feelings and values, love my family. I don't dwell on passing years or diminished physical abilities. I plan to have enough new projects coming in the funnel to keep it full and make the journey fun.

That account pretty well answers the question: how do you sustain your growth? His eloquent statement illustrates the heightened quality of his reflection and a new dimension of his mindfulness, wisdom. His portrait of work, service, growth, and relationships after retirement reflects a successful life. Like others whose stories we have been recounting, El has been redefining success.

Achievement doesn't mean what it did when he was climbing the corporate ladder. He once said, "Success happens everyday when I wake up and realize I have the ability to do whatever I choose and have lots of great things to choose from." On another occasion he wrote that he identified with an author who suggested, "Success is measured by your ability to do what you love and love what you do." El's story captures what success in a fulfilling third age can look like. It matches his epitaph—living the life he has been blessed with to the fullest.

Another aspect to El's becoming the person he can be includes involvement with his family. Their three sons have married and now live close enough so that he and Stephanie can see their families more frequently than when they were scattered. They both enjoy developing relationships with their seven grandchildren. Since their own parents have died, they have become the older generation in their family. To celebrate their expanding family they decided to host a family reunion now that the lodge is fully restored. They invited forty-five family members, who came from New England, Florida, the West Coast, and Alaska. This celebration was a great summertime event, providing a special opportunity to get to know and enjoy one another in an idyllic lake setting in the Maine woods. El and Stephanie have now completed more than forty years of marriage, a relationship that has grown richer and more satisfying through the years. They have been successful in balancing the paradoxical principle of increasing independence and greater intimacy.

During the past sixteen years they have also developed the principle of a more caring life that extends to each other, family, community, the environment, and future generations. In the past few years especially they have expressed concern for children and young people, whom they hope will come to understand and appreciate their environmental values. El has also been learning to care better for himself. He remains physically active in the outdoors and recently committed to a healthy diet. After several months he managed to lose nearly twenty pounds while learning to enjoy new eating habits. As with others we asked: How do you feel about yourself at this time in your life?

So far I'm blessed with good health. If I close my eyes and ask myself how old I am, I'd answer: forty-five! Sure I get tired more easily, wear glasses, and tend to pace myself. But overall I still feel I'm at midlife with a long ways to go. I have the benefit of sixty-three years of experience, with a desire to find more challenges and not rest on past accomplishments or the excuse of being a senior. I do notice a tendency to do things now and not put them off. I don't focus on diminished abilities. If you do, it's easy to rationalize not getting up at three thirty to fish for tarpon or to let the wind blow the leaves away. Some compromises will have to be made eventually. But I have eighty-five-year-old friends who keep me going through the woods.

In his sixties El—like Vic, Ed, and Betty—has continued to lead an active life with a youthful spirit that adds freshness to his mature years. He's embodying the paradox of growing young while growing older. Without being conscious of it, and similar to the other three "retirees," he has chosen the option discussed in chapter 2, that of second growth as an alternative to shriveling in the third age. El is pleased, surprised, and grateful for the way his life has evolved during these sixteen years. If his company could be seen as the place from which he graduated, then he would be a star alumnus. In retrospect he sees that graduation is the right metaphor for taking retirement: "My retirement was a graduation, an event passing from an income-generating activity to a life phase with options, flexibility, satisfaction, and personal and spiritual growth. I don't think of myself as retired, as a stage in life. Rather, I have completed one life phase and moved on to something better."

It is fitting to bring this part of his story to a close with a message he sent us while we were finishing this book:

> After leaving the company I had not yet realized how much growth and renewal there was in store for us. I have so much enjoyed the chance to share my love of the outdoors, especially with youngsters, to leave our environment, fisheries, and wildlife in a better state than I found them, to share the history and traditions of this region with future generations, to love my family more deeply, and to leave a legacy in this region of greater understanding and valuing of our rich outdoor sporting heritage. More recently I have come to recognize that we are blessed by a greater Being with a life that is ours to live wisely and return to him fully lived. I am beginning to see that my journey, my future growth, lies in a more spiritual direction that remains for me to explore more fully.

El's early graduation from the company and subsequent blossoming testifies to the creative potential in each of us to shape a fulfilling life in the third age. Here is another life that puts flesh on the proclamation made by Browning's Rabbi Ben Ezra: "Grow old along with me! The best is yet to be."

FIVE LESSONS FROM GRADUATES

COLLEGES AND UNIVERSITIES CUSTOMARILY INVITE ALUMNI back to share stories with students preparing for life after graduation. As you'll see in chapter 6, some people never leave school; they are still working after all these years and loving it. Others phase out formal work for pay, redefining their lives in semi-retirement. The people whose stories we have told in this chapter have fully retired from their career jobs. What do the experiences of these four successful graduates offer as lessons that you might be able to apply to your life as you prepare for retirement? We see the six principles of growth and renewal operating in their lives. What have these individuals been doing to redefine and reshape retirement and sustain growth? How can you translate their approaches into practical steps to navigate your journey into third age fulfillment?

START WITH YOURSELF

As you look ahead to the next leg in your life journey, it's time to turn inward before considering changing direction. You have a reservoir of creativity within you, largely unnoticed as you have been actively pursuing important goals in your second age. You possess new talents and interests that are waiting to be discovered. Values are shifting and ready to be clarified. Opportunities and adventures wait to be realized. What are they? It's time to explore within.

Practice the art of mindful reflection. Dream a little—dream a lot! Put yourself in a different context within which you're freer to let fresh thoughts enter. Play with them. Share your dreams with your spouse or partner, a close friend, a confidante or coach, or a counselor. Don't be surprised if nothing specific immediately pops into your mind. Creative people know they need a period of aimlessness, a fallow period in which unformed ideas germinate. A psychiatrist who had left his practice six months before, when asked what he was going to do next replied, "I don't know—and that's okay!" Another former leader attending a third age retreat disclosed,

"The only commitment I made to myself when I left the company was that I was going to take a full year to explore what my new options might be; I committed to make no new long-term commitments during that year. I was determined to have that year for reflection."

Vic, Ed, Betty, and El purposefully made themselves open to the unexpected and felt called to something that had not been part of their dream—becoming a caregiver, grieving the loss of a loved one, and discovering an interest in community service. They became open to the future, not knowing what might lie ahead, and thus positioned themselves to respond in ways that eventually enriched their lives.

ONE, TWO, THREE—LET GO!

As you review and contemplate all the good things and achievements that have been integral to your working life during your second age, be prepared to let go. Graduating is often a complex, difficult process, a time to finish activities you've learned to value, to say good-bye to friends, teachers, routines, and familiar situations. It's scary to leave a place where you're known, recognized, and appreciated—like leaving home all over again.

Retirement can be like that, even if you're not thrilled with your current work. Vic had achieved at long last the executive position he wanted and was proud of himself and comfortable in his home and community; but thirty years were enough. He and his wife dreamed of a different kind of life, requiring them to pick up stakes and move on. Ed loved his careers in the university and knew he would miss many close friends and colleagues; but he saw another possibility calling him. Betty was fulfilled by her job, but it was consuming her.

Twelve years were enough. El was outstanding in his high-level finance position; but it was preventing him from fulfilling a dream. Twenty-six years were enough.

In *Misery*, Stephen King introduces a character who asks a European: why did so many Jews stay in Germany when it had become obvious that the Nazi's were intending to kill them? Many Jews, he answered, had developed a great love of music, a passion they tangibly associated with their pianos. They could not leave their pianos; they couldn't imagine life without them. We all have pianos we may be afraid to leave behind. What pianos might be keeping you from letting go? You'll need to clarify what you want in the next phase of your life. What's most important? Review where you've been and what you've got now, and then shift to where you're going and what you dream of becoming? How are your personal attachments, your pianos, preventing you from going for it?

GIVE **IT** A NAME THAT INSPIRES YOU, THAT GUIDES YOU

Naming is a powerful human capability. Remember in Genesis, when God told Adam to name all the animals? A name establishes a personal, emotional connection with what is being named, enables a person to set the framework for an ongoing relationship, and shapes how the person chooses to sustain and grow that relationship. If you are a parent, you remember both the joy and the challenge of choosing a name for a child.

For your retirement, choose a name, a metaphor that will free you to reframe *it* in a personal, inspirational way. Vic's term, graduation, might enthuse you. Other words or phrases might also galvanize you—changing course, protirement, retiring to, starting a new phase in your journey, writing a new chapter in your life, filling your canvas with new sketches, drawings, and paintings. What matters is that you design your life after fifty around core values, interests, and passions, both yours and those of the person, or people, with whom you intend to share your third age. Different from the second age, in which you needed to have clear, concrete goals, for your third age you should set a direction, or directions, not a goal. Think of this step in navigational terms as following a guiding star, or a constellation of stars, as opposed to an X that marks *the* spot.

Goals, especially when written down and publicly shared, do motivate action. But goals also have a way of narrowing a person's focus, closing out alternative possibilities. Indeed, focus was vital to your achievements during the second age. In the third age, however, you are better served by opening yourself up to possibilities likely to be unfamiliar, uncomfortable, and untested. After all, you're entering a new frontier, journeying past known horizons. Life ahead is not going to be like the life you've had. You must see things with a realistic optimism to keep yourself going forward—but just where you're headed is initially not necessarily going to be known. But, not to worry, you won't fall off the edge. One participant in a third age retreat commented, "I don't know where I'm going, but I'm sure it's the right direction."

Retirement as conventionally conceived could anchor you forever in a safe harbor, tinkling on the eighty-eight keys of your piano. There's a big ocean out there. Your graduation will launch you into uncharted waters. The message of your commencement is: *go for* IT!

Get Started on Your Portfolio and Keep on Painting

We have been using another metaphor along the way—building a third age life portfolio. In chapter 3 we posed a list of questions to help you get started in building your portfolio; and in chapter 7 we'll have much more to say about this idea. Your aim, we suggest, is to use your guiding star, the fire in your soul, and your creative capacities to build a more enriched, complex life than you've had till now. Truly creative people develop complex lives.

Your life portfolio will be the practical way for you to define your evolving identity during your third age. Your life portfolio expresses who you are becoming. Now is the time to attend to what you love and most care about—for spouse or partner, for family, and for friends; for your own health, wellbeing, and spirituality; for community and nature; for discovery, learning, work, play, and adventure; for beauty, children, and laughter.

The secret in putting together a third age life portfolio involves balancing multiple interests and commitments. Balance the paradoxes of second growth at every turn along the way. Take more time to turn into yourself. Pay attention to people and issues that matter. You will become conscious of more opportunities to expand and realize your dreams. You may have developed so many different interests that you have wondered how you'll find time for all of them; yet you'll be amazed at the freedom you have to shape each day as you choose.

As Vic learned, building a life portfolio is like working on a huge canvas. Don't worry about filling it up; just keep the work in progress. Each sunrise presents you with another section of your grand canvas. Keep on painting.

FIGURE OUT WHAT SUCCESS LOOKS LIKE **FOR YOU**

As you see your commencement into the third age taking you in exciting, new directions, you'll need to develop for yourself new measures of success. Success in the second age often happened through concentrated focusing on and reaching distinct goals, often organizational objectives that may or may not have been aligned with your passions and aspirations.

Success within the process of building a third age life portfolio lies in the quality of your unfolding life. In the third age, success will have more to do with living your life to the fullest, doing what you love and loving what you do, leaving a legacy of which you can be proud, that gives you a sense of meaning and purpose. In short, during the second age most measures of success are external and involve principally how other people judge the merit of your actions. Remember the report cards you got in school? How about those appraisals of performance at work? And peer rankings? How many people on their deathbeds will say, "Gee, I wish I had gotten just one more 360-degree assessment."

In the third age, your measures of success will mainly come from inside yourself. Learn to trust in how you yourself treasure the contributions you are making, rather than in how others assess the worth of what you are doing. A question we often pose to those sharing their stories has been: what makes your soul sing? If you don't hear your soul singing, you need to go back to lesson one and start over. What do you want in life now? Are you headed in that direction? In those directions? When you are finally on your way, stop, turn off the noise inside your own head, and listen to the music your soul is making. Keep on painting, keep on listening. Keep on going for IT.

CHAPTER FIVE

SERENDIPITY

Where are the songs of Spring? Aye, where are they?

Think not of them, thou hast thy music too—

—KEATS, *"To Autumn"*

EXPECT THE UNEXPECTED

PEOPLE WHO WELCOME RETIREMENT as a graduation from second age careers to a new way of living and working in the third age have prepared for the next phase in their lives with mindful reflection and planning. As illustrated in the last chapter, this preparation enables them to start projects they have been dreaming about, seek new adventures, sometimes move to a more desirable location, or change lifestyles to provide more appropriate challenges and greater satisfaction. The results of new developments are pleasantly surprising. When asked what he thought of aging after turning a hundred, the comedian George Burns quipped, "Well, it's better than the alternative." For many people life after fifty is turning out to be better than any alternative they could imagine. But it doesn't always start out that way.

Some people in our study have been more than a little surprised, perceiving their evolving lives paradoxically, not so much as fulfilling expectations, but as exceeding them. They often tell us they had no idea that their change of course would take them to where they are now: "I didn't expect the next phase would be so exciting." Failures and detours sometimes block the course; but they can become pathways to fulfillment: "Thank heavens I didn't get what I thought I wanted. This is so much better." Accidents and misfortune in retrospect sometimes lead to something beneficial. Losses can result in unexpected gains: "I felt a lot of pain, but when I recovered I was in a much better space." Against enormous odds, some people experience exceptionally happy outcomes. Our research has repeatedly uncovered a recurring paradox. Not only are the best things in life free, but they also sometimes drop in without warning. In short, the experience of serendipity can transform the most carefully planned lives. This profound paradox offers a crucial lesson for anyone preparing for retirement, especially when that retirement entails loss of valued activities, interests, and relationships, and the meaning that derives from them.

Other studies have stumbled upon unexpected surprises occurring after people retire. In his book bringing to conclusion a seventy-year longitudinal study of American lives, John Clausen described a remarkable change in one man. For thirty years he had been a highly competent, conscientious, successful lawyer. At fifty-five he had identified himself with his career and had scored the highest possible rating for satisfaction with work. Since adolescence he had known exactly what he wanted to do. A few years later, as he reflected on what he might want to do next with his life, he grew less certain. At fifty-nine he sensed a need to change course. Having previously ended a long marriage with divorce, he broke completely from his carefully crafted professional career. He indulged in what he called "hedonism" by devoting himself to reading great books, traveling, and learning French. He also entered into a new relationship with a woman who was twenty years younger and who was developing a flourishing law practice as he was ending his. Clausen was amazed at this unexpected transformation of a person who had heretofore modeled conservative values and conventional success.

In another book that drew on results from three different longitudinal studies on aging, George Vaillant reports surprising developments among retired people. A former physical education teacher started violin lessons at sixty-five and began a musical career that was going strong when he checked in with her at seventy-eight. A retired businessman got so bored with retirement that he risked an entirely different line of work, and was flourishing as a magazine editor in his late seventies. A couple of men, both teachers who had appeared to be declining into dullness at fifty, took early retirement and found the courage to release suppressed talents. They dedicated themselves to developing and expressing their creativity through the arts and new projects in retirement. In their midseventies they were so exuberant, transformed, and fulfilled that Vaillant seemed amazed.

While Clausen and Vaillant found remarkable outcomes occasionally, we believe these examples are harbingers of things to come with Baby Boomers. Other studies report on cohorts considerably older than those in our study. People in our study are relearning a childhood capacity to relish surprises. As you grow young while growing older, you shall see possibilities more readily. Your eyes will appreciate the randomness of surprises that burst forth like wild flowers in early spring. Many people in our study have been experiencing the happy surprises of serendipity in the third age. You might also do so, if you learn to "play it right."

Playing it right means promoting second growth in your third age. As described in chapter 3, this venture involves discovering and releasing your potential creativity to shape a meaningful, fulfilling mature life. As you navigate your life into the future, you have to adopt a creative mentality. You may not think of yourself as creative—so far. But years of experience, learning, and your own development have stocked your personal resources with potential. Your task now is to become sensitive to what lies within and what can be. Storm your brain for this potential and the not-yet-experienced. Embrace the dream that hasn't yet become a reality, and risk putting it on the map. Your third age challenges you to grow creatively, and by responding to this challenge you shall make the creative ordinary. Creativity will become both an *input to* and an *output of* your second growth. Yes, another paradox to expect and accept.

. We can take as our models creative people who have been not only making new things, but also making themselves new. In a five-year study of ninety-one creative individuals, most of them over sixty and representing many fields—arts, humanities, science, business, and politics—psychologist Mihaly Csikszentmihalyi learned how they were delighted with the surprises that emerged in their lives. Creativity, the work of discovering and designing something new, involves imagination and reflection, risk and challenge, commitment and persistence, patience and resolve. The result, he found, is not only a recognized contribution in their fields of endeavor, but also an enrichment of a personal life.

Creative people love what they do. Their lives are filled with the experience of flow, a total, integrating engagement in an appropriate challenge in which talents are developed, concentration is intense, and time seems to stop. In flow, people experience their optimal selves, and in these special moments their souls sing. Creative individuals often make the pleasantly incredulous discovery that they personally have changed in the process. Csikszentmihalyi believes the experience of creative people should encourage us all to tap our creative potential and engage in a creative quest that will make our lives exciting and worthwhile. We agree. You can express your creativity by redefining your life, your work, and your retirement.

Eva: *The biggest task is to find my way towards another way.*

When Eva retired at sixty-five, she could never have predicted how her life would unfold. Three years later she told an impressive story of serendipity. In her youth she had been a good student, majoring in psychology at Stanford, where she also acted in theatrical productions. After getting a master's degree in clinical psychology, she integrated her love of theater with counseling to develop a career in the new fields of psychodrama and family therapy. Her first marriage to a poet-musician ended after fifteen years because he did not want children and she did. Her second marriage to Alan, a psychiatrist, established an enduring family with two grown sons and a grandson. Eva also collaborated with her husband in building a therapy practice. After giving birth, she combined private practice, teaching, book writing, and motherhood. In her early fifties she decided to challenge herself by taking a different career track: she went into teaching nearly fulltime in a graduate program.

Few people were aware that this attractive, creative, professional Californian had been born in Germany and raised in

Berlin during World War II. Eva's mother was Gentile; her Jewish father escaped to San Francisco at the last moment. Eva and her mother remained in Berlin, enduring the bombings and hunger until the end of the war. In 1946 at age eleven she and her mother caught the first boat to San Francisco to join her father. Soon after she settled in America, her father died; her mother, who had become an alcoholic, died a few years later. Growing up in America, Eva kept her German past separate from her new life. Only in her midfifties, when she began to write a memoir for her family did the German and American roles begin to merge. As she started writing about her wartime experiences as a young girl, she found a way to talk about stories long stored in her mind, shared only with her German friends. She then began to think about expanding her memoirs into another book.

After eleven years of teaching, while launching this new book project, she had a serious accident—a bad fall down stairs, with a heavy picture crashing down on her head. This accident precipitated her move into retirement and also caused her debilitating, chronic pain for over a year. The mishap had a profound effect on her life and on her personal identity. Eva had always been energetic, active, and productive, but during the first year after the accident she could do little. After trying several healing methods without much success, she reluctantly agreed to have surgery, a procedure that improved her situation but required a ten-month recovery. During this convalescence she could do almost nothing, because any movement resulted in severe pain. She used much of her time to reflect on her life, and eventually she was able to perceive her fall not only as a disaster but also as an opportunity.

The fall gave her a gift of freedom—time to explore hidden dimensions in herself and to discover her potential for

new experiences. It also gave her a much-needed message—
to slow down. Reflection and a slower pace sparked creativity that had been lying fallow deep within her. While adapting
to a long recovery, the accident appeared to her as a gateway
to a different way of living.

Because of this fall, my situation changed quite a bit. It
has been important for me to fully recognize and accept
the fact that I had this fall that hurt my neck and required
surgery with a long recovery. This changed my life. I've
been an optimistic and energetic individual. I just couldn't
see myself as the kind of person I'd become, an invalid. I
had to stop doing just about everything. Even reading
was difficult. I tried everything, hoping to avoid surgery.
I'm nearly recovered now, but it took two years. All that
time I was handicapped. I kept thinking: how am I going
to handle being handicapped? This is my life. You know,
chronic pain is so boring. I was always complaining. I had
to push it away—you can do it. The consequences of the
fall meant I was totally retired. I had to figure out what
this might mean.

As Eva began to feel stronger, she was able to rediscover
her resilience. Recalling aspects of herself in the past, she
began to record her memories and explore a past that she
had set aside. In doing so she has created a new, different
sense of herself, one that she believes is more appropriate for
her third age.

The fall hurt, not just physically but psychologically. The
whole experience was hard. But it had a positive side. It
taught me to rediscover myself. And it improved my optimism. I had always been optimistic. But when I didn't feel
better, I got discouraged. Recovery was slow. A little bit

after three months—then a little more after six months.
My doctor said I was doing well, but I was still in terrible
pain. I went to physical therapy regularly. And I talked
with everyone I could. Sharing my problem helped. I
didn't have a goal, but I had a vague picture of my life as
I wanted it to unfold. I imagined that the last half of life
should be quieter than the first. I never wanted to be one
of those people who press hard right up to the end. I
wanted to become a person who had time for creativity—
to think, to draw, to develop my garden, and become
more spiritual.

The changes she was making in her life as a result of the
fall and her prolonged recovery led her to a new insight. In
retrospect, her accident had provided an entrance into a new
way of living. Eva wasn't yet sure what all this new way would
entail, but she had a firm sense that she was experiencing a
big spurt of creativity. She thinks that perhaps many people
over fifty need something to wake them up—an external
event to knock them off course, to provoke the discovery of
the richness within them and the creative possibilities in
front of them.

A couple of years after her fall, while making progress on
her book, Eva came to another realization. Not only was she
discovering another dimension of herself, she was also integrating her German identity with the American side of her
life, something she had never been able to do before. This
deep integration of two different aspects of her being was
another gift of the fall. This integration soon sent her in an
unexpected direction into a third age career. Never having
taught in Germany, she began teaching family therapy and
psychodrama there, where she found her books widely read.
She was surprised to discover how readily she recovered use
of her native tongue. Back in California she began doing a

new kind of work, reconciliation workshops with adults who had experienced the horrors of war either personally or through their parents. They, too, had been searching for ways to come to terms with a painful past and to integrate suppressed fragments into present understanding. At sixty-nine her new career includes teaching both at home and abroad, therapy, writing, and even a major role in a documentary film about German children in World War II.

As she shapes her new work, she also finds herself trying to redefine retirement.

My attitude towards retirement has been changing. I didn't think much about what it would mean. I was never the type of person who said: I'll move to Florida or build a little house with a picket fence. I've always found things to do that I've wanted to do. The most important thing right now is to figure out what it means to retire. I'm 90 percent recovered, but I don't want to go back to teaching. My husband still works about three-quarters time in his seventies. He owns his practice and has control of his work. He's starting to take more time off. I'm looking for another way, one less scheduled. The main difference with my life now is that I can write, study, do workshops in Germany, travel, garden, and spend more time being a wife, a role that I'm appreciating more than ever, now that I have time for it. I'm not sure what's coming, but I know it will be much different than what I've known. I have a friend who's been retired twenty years who said, "I can finally take a nap without feeling guilt." I'm not there yet. I still feel guilty if I'm not productive. But I'm productive in different ways. I've never spent so much time in my home. I notice my house much more—also my garden. I keep trying to make my home and garden more beautiful. Work is still important, but it's different. My work now is whatever I'm working on. And much of it is being creative.

What's next? It's the creative stuff. I've always been creative. Now, more so. I cook. I garden. I teach. I don't go to
work, but I'm working—and working on what work means.
It's hard to get rid of the notion that I should always be
productive. I grew up thinking that way. The biggest task
is to find my way to another way.

Initially, Eva's fulltime retirement resulted from her neck
injury. As it is for many people, it was a time to bring a career
to an end. Later, in response to an external event that she at
first experienced as a great setback, she began to redesign
her life, a process that has led to her exploring the meaning
of retirement. It marks, as she said, a time to become a more
creative person. Since recovering from the accident, Eva
seems to be building a third age life portfolio comprised of a
mix of her important interests: different kinds of work; ample
time for learning; play and creativity; building stronger relationships with her husband, family, and friends; contributing
to the community; developing spirituality and a closer relationship with nature; and taking care of herself. Applying her
creativity to her own life, she is finding a way that is qualitatively and quantitatively different from anything she had previously known or even imagined.

The surprisingly positive outcome of her painful fall,
which knocked her off her intended direction after retirement,
resulted in large part from the resilience and resourcefulness
she eventually discovered within herself. Resilience sprang
from the optimism she mustered, which sustained her recovery and growth. Resourcefulness came from honest recognition and acceptance of the pain and loss she experienced,
combined with her struggle to work through the suffering
until it becomes meaningful. She repeatedly affirms that the
mishap has been a gift. What an extraordinary serendipity
and personal transformation.

She tells another story that illustrates how she has been using her creativity to express pain, find new meaning, and achieve integration. Soon after Eva had retired, a former student contacted her, because she had been unable to work through deep, prolonged grief at the death of her mother. This woman had previously been part of a course Eva offered, in which students staged a part of their lives. She felt that Eva might help her come to terms with her recent loss. While listening to her former student, Eva was aware of her own grief: her best friend of fifty years—they had become friends in high school—had just died from cancer. Eva realized that she, too, had grief that needed to be transformed.

> So we agreed that we needed to arrange a performance, a psychodrama to work through the grief. We started gathering various aspects of our lives that related to our grief. My former student was Mexican; she had cultural ideas and artifacts to include. We made a plywood coffin that was a big part of our performance. We included poems, music, and movement in our performance, which we performed here in my garden. We called it, *covered with ashes*. About forty people attended and participated. Psychodrama provides a way to express yourself. My friend felt that losing a mother is like losing a part of yourself. I felt the same with the loss of my best friend. This dramatic expression of grieving was a way towards healing and transformation. We weaved together in this drama memories of her mother and my friend, as well as other losses. We did a dance with ashes. Afterwards people joined in singing and carrying candles. This was such a great experience for us—a way of recovery and reaffirmation.

In staging her expression of grief, Eva tapped theatrical talents that had been dormant for years. She was also engaged in a process of integration, weaving strands of memory, pain, love, and creativity into her emerging personal identity. The women compiled a booklet of photos, a program, and mementos. The album symbolized a part of her that she wanted to integrate into the person she would become. As we have said before, growth through the third age is paradoxical: a complex mixture of pain and exhilaration, grief and joy, loss and discovery, doubt and affirmation. This growth process yields a richer, more complex, more integrated personality.

At seventy, Eva feels that she is both older and youthful. Her self-description as she ages is filled with paradoxes:

> Is this old age? Yes and no. I know I'm aging—I need new glasses, my strength is not what it was, I get tired earlier. I'm more vulnerable. It's also sad, as a woman, to lose your looks when you were attractive. It's also sad to lose good friends who have died. There's no way to replace them. That's part of being older. But I think I can still be young. There's lots of way to be old. I have a friend who's eighty-eight. She's slowed down a lot, but her spirit, language, and attitude are youthful. I expect to be that way. I know I'm youthful. I hope I can remain youthful for a long time. I have returned to aerobic dance. I'm still flexible. I once taught a course on death and dying. I've been giving a good deal of thought to this passage, too. I'm trying to find my way through this part of life, trying to understand death and dying, and to remain optimistic and youthful. I think I have many years ahead. I'm aiming at 104. Why? Something about that number appeals to me.

Eva's creative work in moving her life forward reflects the six principles we find operative in third age growth and renewal. While radically changing her previous mode of operation, she has continued to be mindfully reflective, trying out new ways, strengthening her optimism, and building a positive third age identity incorporating the paradox of growing older/growing young. Conscious of her aging, she has at the same time reaffirmed a youthful spirit that infuses her daily activities. Eva resumed energetic activities as soon as she was able. She takes care of herself, striving to maintain health as a foundation for successful aging. She takes pleasure in her home, cooks, and gardens. A large, robust rose-filled garden in front of her home sees much of her during most of the year. In the last report she said, "It's taken me five years, but I've finally understood my garden." She does aerobic exercises several times a week, and once a week she goes off with good friends on a two-hour to three-hour hike up and down steep Marin County hills. Older friends who have become sedentary and seemingly achy inspire her to stay active.

As well as keeping her body fit, Eva exercises her sharp, critical mind. In addition to the reading and writing related to her new career, she reads poetry, studies art, listens to music, and keeps up with the news. She has many friends of all ages and uses the freedom of more time to be with them. She also gives more time to her family. Both sons now live nearby, and her first grandchild gives her much pleasure. While caring for herself, she is expanding the caring she gives others.

Eva's growth is not only creative, but also spiritual. She has always been a spiritual person, but developing her spirituality has become more important.

My spirituality has been a part of me all my life. I've always had a kind of pantheistic faith in nature. I wasn't raised in the Jewish tradition. As a teenager in the United States I became a Lutheran. After I got confirmed, I felt that I didn't need to go to church. I had learned the principles. I had a sense of ethics and spirit. What appeals most to me now is Buddhism. I practice meditation. Everyday I spend time in reflection and prayer. Sometimes I go off on a retreat. I've done Sufi practices, studied Native American spirituality, and done body movement. I can stand Quaker meetings, but I don't like services and sermons. Most recently I've been memorizing lots of poems and prayers. This is an increasingly important part of my life now.

Like many others in our study, Eva has been personalizing her spirituality, trying to find her own way on a course of continuing growth. What's next? She sees much more freedom stretching before her, offering her opportunities to understand more deeply the process of living and dying and to expand her creativity. Living has once again become a thrilling adventure filled with many things that make her soul sing. What things? "Poetry, music, and art; travel, discovery, and friends; my children, my grandchild, and babies in general; flowers, birds, gardening, and my cat, whose purring helped so much in recovery." Eva's change of course goes on, and will continue to evolve for decades before she reaches her intended destination of 104.

Woody: I find this arrangement so satisfactory that I'm absolutely convinced that if I were offered my half-time job back, I'd say, no. Really!

When interviewed twenty years ago for The Third Age, Woody, at fifty, was president of a small New York City–based company that provided contract and labor negotiation services to healthcare organizations. Trained as a lawyer, he found this work challenging and satisfying, but at the time he was downsizing his work schedule to attend to other important matters. During his forties he had taken Outward Bound courses that led to a personal transformation. Although he had never been athletic, he discovered how much fun he could have climbing, backpacking, canoeing, and kayaking. During his forties and early fifties he had been striving to put more play into his life. By delegating responsibilities to people he had been developing, he realized that he could accomplish his leadership goals in a forty-hour week. He was balancing work and play.

He was also redefining work: volunteering on boards, contributing to the community, doing adjunct teaching, and learning. Woody was proud of his contributions to the formation of a new kind of Outward Bound school in New York City, bringing together urban youth with professionals in local programs. By his midfifties he felt he was riding the crest of a wave. Life had never been better. He and his wife had a good marriage; their two daughters were turning out well; they had many friends; they were traveling more, sometimes to exotic places like China and India; he was in good health and learning new skills, like scuba diving; his work relationships were pleasant and his professional stature was receiving recognition. His evolving life modeled second growth. At fifty-five he mentioned that several friends had lost their jobs because of a recession, and he hoped he would never have to face such an ordeal. Fate determined otherwise.

With the onset of a recession, his board decided it was time for a change. Pushed out of his position, Woody received a golden parachute for a year to find other work. Nothing appropriate or suitable seemed available to someone his age. While he was searching for employment, the New York Outward Bound School urged him to assist in their development. After doing pro bono consulting, they asked him if he would consider becoming its associate director. The pay was low, but he and his wife realized they could get by on less, now that their home was paid for and their daughters had finished their educations. He decided to take on this new adventure. After five years, at sixty-three, he was again riding high. He loved his new job.

> I still work hard and love every minute of it. The best thing is variety. I never know what I'll be doing when I walk in the door. I may meet with corporate executives, conduct teambuilding training, work with teachers, participate in activities with kids, or help keep our computers on line. When I left my old job, part of the severance package included outplacement support, where I described my dream job. In retrospect, it nearly defines what I'm doing now. The organization considers itself a learning organization, and I consider myself a learner. Most of the staff is young; I'm the oldest by ten years. I kid about losing my hair and how old I am. But I don't feel old and would like to think I'm not considered old.

Like others we have interviewed, Woody has learned to call upon his creative resources when confronting a major challenge, and to redefine his work to suit the way he wants to live: life-centered work rather than a work-centered life. One reason he could make this adjustment so well is because he was already redefining what success meant. It wasn't to be measured by externals—position, fame, income, or even power. Shortly before being pushed out as company president he said,

> What's success mean? How can I put it? I lead a life of contrasts. I'm president of a good company. I'm publicly involved. I've helped start an exciting program for kids. I'm into outdoor activities, traveling to unusual places, teaching, and spending time with family and friends. I play many different roles. What I would like people to say

about me is that I lead an exciting life, that I'm venture-some, a man of many sides. I'm trying to make an interesting life.

Woody had been making a good living, but meaning, he realized, comes from the totality of his life. His goal was to create an interesting life, a life portfolio. He learned that by leaving his executive position he did not leave behind the opportunity for leadership. Like other third agers in our study, he was making a difference both within and outside of his organization. But he set all this rebalancing within the framework of developing his potential, redefining his work, having more fun in hobbies and outdoor activities, expanding areas of learning, and strengthening relationships with family and friends. Success, he found, was to flow from this complex process, though he was also proud and pleased with public recognition for his contributions. At sixty-seven he was still making an interesting life.

I work fulltime for Outward Bound and continue to love every minute of it. Each day offers new challenges and projects. The latest is a major move. We bought our own building. It's old, and I'm in charge of renovation. This involves architects, engineers, contractors, and lots of hands-on stuff, like climbing the scaffolding. My job, through my making, has lots of flexibility. I do work at home on my PC and am out of the office a lot, mostly facilitating corporate teambuilding programs in various locations. I keep active and feel well. I'm finding there's little I want to do that I can't. We don't worry about money. We seem to have enough to do what we want in a modest way. I enjoy being with our grandchildren. And my latest interest is in a digital camera and in learning to master my new PC.

Woody had been manifesting a zest for life for over seventeen years, fully involved in work, family, and community. He has been carrying a sense of adventure into multiple areas, even though he had been set back on several occasions in the previous ten years—the loss of a leadership position, a daughter's divorce, and his wife's illness. The divorce, with his daughter's burden of becoming a single mom, saddened him, but it also inspired him to spend more time with her and her two children. His wife recovered, and, as we've seen, his job loss turned into an unexpected gain. Woody was showing no signs of reigning in. So what was he thinking about retirement?

The following year we explored this question with him. He had remained fully active in his job, but he had made a slight adjustment. Facing a deteriorating financial status, New York Outward Bound had been forced to make salary cuts and layoffs. Woody had seen this staff reduction as an opportunity to gain more freedom and flexibility in his life, and so he had agreed to cut back to a four-day week, an arrangement perceived as an improvement. The reduced workweek was giving him both greater freedom and more flexibility so that he had more chances to pursue other interests and adventures. However, at sixty-nine he was not seeing retirement as an option for him: "I love what I do in this job. I have no thoughts of retiring. How do I feel about retirement? Frankly, it scares the hell out of me. I'd like to stay working here for twenty more years until they carry me out. I see an active life for me as long as possible."

In retrospect, he was on the verge of exploring a semiretired lifestyle. His wife's condition had improved, and so they could travel, and they had just returned from a trip to the Baltic that they enjoyed tremendously. He had also been spending more time with his oldest grandson, who at thirteen was learning scuba diving so he could join his grandfather in underwater adventures. They did a diving certification program together. "We formed a great pair. I'm ready for adventure, wherever it comes." It seemed that we weren't yet going to learn much from Woody about redefining retirement. "Put it off as long as possible" seemed to be his motto.

Early the next year Woody reported that cutting back to four days had been a wonderful decision. He was able to meet his goals at work, but in addition he had more free time to be with his family. He and his wife were doing more traveling. This happy situation was not destined to last, for after several months the organization's financial situation was worsening.

> When things did not improve, my work schedule was cut
> to half time—not my decision. But once again I found
> that I had no trouble occupying my time and quickly
> began to appreciate that schedule, too. Then, about six
> months ago: the shocker. My job was eliminated along
> with another one. I was initially devastated and unsure of
> how I would spend my time and find excitement, stimula-
> tion, and enough to do.

Once again what he had dreaded became a reality. In his case, being forced to retire at sixty-nine was not a severe financial threat, because he and his wife had managed to save enough. The threat was to his sense of meaning and his redefinition of success. How was he going to go on making an interesting life?

As he had before, Woody reflected on what he loved most about what he had lost and started thinking about how he could fill the gap. To retain excitement and find meaning, some retired people he had observed were doing volunteer work that engaged them. Woody had volunteered on projects before, as well as to this organization during the past thirteen years he had been employed. He treasures the work this organization does for young people and society. It has made a significant difference in the lives of thousands of young people. Why not continue to support it by volunteering?

> I surprised everyone at Outward Bound by offering to continue my half-time position as a volunteer. My offer was readily accepted. In appreciation the organization agreed to pay my benefits. About a month into the new arrangement, they decided to pay me a small annual honorarium. I continue to do all the things I did before as a half-timer, with the same title, responsibility, and authority. I put in somewhat less time in the office. Since I don't have a nine-to-five obligation, I commute less. Because I can do so much of the work at home with e-mail, phone, and fax, I can avoid the rush hour commute and drive to work in less time.
>
> I find this arrangement so satisfactory that I'm absolutely convinced that if I were offered my half-time job back, I'd say, no. Really! My life is good. My days are full and I wonder how I ever could have done all the things I now do while I was working half time. My wife and I just returned from an adventuresome vacation to Prague, Budapest, Vienna, and Salzburg. And we're thinking about a family trip next year to celebrate my seventieth birthday. I'm experiencing a happy and fulfilling version of semiretirement.

Upon losing his job, Woody had fallen into the retirement pit that had scared him. He didn't want to be in the space into which he had been pushed. By responding to this challenge with creativity, resourcefulness, and a strong measure of optimism, he was able to redefine retirement in a way that enabled him to pursue his distinctive version of success. His unexpected outcome was another serendipity. A year later Woody reported, "I couldn't be happier." He wouldn't change back to a regular work schedule. In fact, he was offered another fulltime assignment with lots of travel, and he turned it down. He did accept a consulting engagement in his old field of healthcare labor relations, and is open to more such opportunities. But he will not sacrifice the freedom, flexibility, and stimulating challenges he's finding in retirement, though he doesn't use that term to describe his situation. He continues to be as involved as ever as an Outward Bound volunteer, and believes he is almost as productive as he was when officially working half time. With greater flexibility, he and his wife can travel more often to be with their grandchildren. To celebrate turning seventy, he's taking his wife and two adult daughters to Turkey for the first time. And he's joined the YMCA, working out several times a week and once a week with a trainer. Woody still succeeds in making an interesting life.

In the serendipity of unexpected semiretirement Woody has not abandoned his impressive leadership role. On the contrary, he continues to practice what Peter Drucker has called "leading beyond the walls." Drucker argues that society desperately needs people actively engaged in the social sector, activists who contribute their expertise, energy, and spirit to support the wellbeing of the community. Flexibility in work schedules, with a redefined retirement, provides opportunity for third agers to develop new forms of leadership that serve society and the future. Woody has chosen to continue his leadership role on a volunteer basis, becoming an accomplished *social entrepreneur.* For this voluntary leadership he receives recognition and appreciation. This past year he was given Outward Bound's system-wide staff recognition award, presented at the annual board meeting of all the schools, a much-treasured honor as he turns seventy. Woody is another example of a person who keeps developing his own distinctive version of a third age career in semiretirement; he also shows the serendipity that is possible in the creative reinvention of retirement.

Rebecca: *Passion for me is the most important thing. My art is an expression of my spirituality and my passion. It's who I am—a self-portrait. If I didn't get to do that, I would get depressed.*

Entering Rebecca's lovely home in San Francisco is like stepping into an exquisite small art museum. Paintings and photos cover the walls of every room, hallway, and stairwell, and tables and shelves hold sculptures and ceramics. The artwork comes in all sizes, styles, textures, and forms. You'd think she were a collector, until she tells you modestly that over the past thirty years she has created most of what you see. A small woman with curly white hair, dark framed glasses, and a bright red sweater, she—like her art—stands out as a study in contrasts: vivacious and reflective, energetic and soulful, artistic and practical, passionate and restrained. She and her husband have lived in this house for over forty years, investing energy, creativity, and love into a carefully designed space that expresses who they are and what they care about. Although Rebecca has experienced several serendipities in her seventy-five years, she observes that what she is experiencing now is the best: "This is the best time for me. I'm fortunate—my husband, too. We don't have health problems, so we have opportunities to do our passionate stuff."

Rebecca was born in a small town in Oklahoma, where her dad owned a small store. When the depression hit, he moved his family to Texas so he could work for an oil company. Encouraged by her mother and grandmother, she developed her talents as a dancer from an early age and later got involved in stage productions—dancing, singing, and acting—both in high school and in college. She finished a drama degree at the University of Texas, where she also worked on productions and set design. After graduation she took a job as an assistant director with the student union, which put on shows for special occasions. She thought she had found her niche.

But after breaking up with a boyfriend, she went home to her parents, who had moved to Arkansas. While there, thinking about what she would do next, she was asked to perform in a benefit production for a heart fund. In the audience was a visitor recently arrived in this country. Entranced by her singing and dancing, he sent roses backstage, came to meet her, and soon proposed. As a Jew involved in the Jewish community and a refugee who fled from the Nazis, he asked if she would consider converting. She agreed, and they were married four months later. She has been making a Jewish home ever since, and they have been happily married nearly fifty years. Serendipity number one!

Rebecca's husband finished an MBA on the East Coast and took a job that moved them to San Francisco. As they were getting established and starting to have children, the company collapsed. With no income and little savings, her husband started a small investment firm to help entrepreneurs, and soon realized that he was entrepreneurial. He founded a mail order company that became successful on a national scale. Another serendipity. What enabled her to make this transition through some lean years, she said, was a practical optimism.

I've always been optimistic. I didn't worry about what would happen. I'm the ideal wife for an entrepreneur. I take risks. That's what I live on, risk taking. When friends would express concern that I didn't have anything set early in our marriage, I would say to them: this is an adventure. That's an important word for me. I look on what's coming next as an adventure. I'm not big on putting on shows, but right now I'm working with a photographer to put my work in a jury situation. That's a risk—but one worth taking.

While managing their home and raising children, Rebecca took her first painting course at a Jewish Community Center, where her teacher told her that she belonged at the Art Institute. She waited a few years before taking courses in painting and sculpture there. After she had her third child, her husband encouraged her to use her practical and creative talents to develop merchandising for the company. Although Rebecca had no retail experience, she designed a plan to become a fulltime merchandising manager in her husband's firm while still being a wife and mother. Learning the business came naturally, she said, like working in a production for a theater: helping with layouts, arranging for photographers and models, and doing buying. She traveled to New York and Europe to keep the company on the cutting edge, continued to be a wife and mother, and took more classes at the Art Institute. For years she juggled priorities and enjoyed doing so. It was a new adventure.

At fifty-eight, after twenty years as a manager, she decided to change course by leaving the company to focus on other aspects of her life. She did not view her departure as an early retirement, because for her it was time to devote more energy to expressing her passions. Disliking the term *retirement* then and now, she and her husband together and individually have been redefining retirement, a long, ongoing process that has taken fifteen years—so far.

> The **R** word is not in our vocabulary. Why? Well, retirement doesn't seem to be much fun. What we're doing is more fun. Work is still an important part of my life—and my husband's. But our work is redefined. It's not for money. Money makes following your passion difficult. You have to have it, but if it guides your life, it's going to eat you up. That's why I'm not interested in selling my art. I have sold to some people. I'm wrestling with this. I should be willing to show my art—I have, but perhaps not as much as I should. I'm thinking, after thirty years of painting I should show more. I'm taking steps now to do that—it's one way to get better at it.

In this new period, Rebecca and her husband were also redefining their identities. They have been changing focus to clarify and express core values that have become more important to them as they've grown older.

> We're both passionate about our identities. Mine has been focused on becoming more creative. My husband has been passionate about becoming creative in his own way. He sold the last part of his mail order company a few years ago. He continues to work; but instead of making money, he works to give it away. He founded a nonprofit. He's also written three books—to help people start their own businesses, and he's just finished his autobiography. And he's been passionately involved in a Jewish community in Scandinavia. He's been invited to join old friends he's known since he was a boy; they're building a Jewish museum there, and he's raising money for that. In doing this, he's reviving relationships that have become his extended family. We're looking forward to traveling there for the opening.

Neither Rebecca nor her husband considered the cessation of income-producing work as retirement. It has been a change of course that has freed them to pursue dreams that only gradually crystallized. New horizons still beckon; they have yet to drop anchor. When Rebecca left the company, her first priority was her art. Having taken classes over several years, she had been able to learn and experiment with different styles and media. Finally able to express fully her newly discovered talent for artwork, she was recasting her identity as a creative person:

> I am highly creative person. I see my life now as creative. If I didn't have this creative aspect in my life, I would just shrivel up and disappear. My art is an expression of my spirituality and my passion. Art is a self-portrait—an instrument to express yourself. If I don't get to work for a period of time, I get depressed. When I look around my house and see my work, I know that's who I am.

Many of Rebecca's paintings, sculptures, and ceramics vividly express her love of life, celebrating people, flowers, animals, landscapes, and bright colors. Her palate has been mostly red, orange, and yellow: "Watch out for red, the books and critics tell me—but just let me express it." But not all her art is celebratory. Some forms express pain, anguish, and grief. Several large, unfinished canvasses in her workshop are painted in black, dark blue, and purple to express her feelings about 9/11, terrorism, and war. And in her dining room she showed the video of an artistic expression of grief in which she mourned the death of her oldest son.

Rebecca's son, a diabetic, had died at forty-two from a staph infection. She and her husband were grief stricken. Devastated, he at once wept and mourned deeply, but

Rebecca's more complicated grieving took longer. In such terrible pain that she wondered how she could go on, she found a gifted grief counselor with whom she worked for over a year. Later, while attending a Day of the Dead celebration in Mexico, she experienced a connection between her life and formidable symbols of the dead that inspired her to try something new. Later, on a Pacific beach near her home, she worked through her grief in an artistic venue that included painting, movement, and sculpture. With several friends she enacted this living art form and filmed the ceremony as a way of remembering their son and the grief that has been integrated into their lives. The full range of her art shows that her passion includes joy and grief, love and sorrow, and above all, gratitude for the fullness of life she experiences. Her art serves as a montage portrait of a person who continues to change and grow more complex.

Rebecca is also passionate about tennis. When she quit her manager's job, she took tennis lessons for the first time and learned that she had the coordination, stamina, and flexibility to play well. She practiced and played nearly every day. In her early sixties she became part of an over-sixty women's team that started to win tournaments. At sixty-eight Rebecca was captain of that team when it won a national championship. Still playing in the Super Senior Tennis League (over sixty-five), she considers staying fit important. She used to run as well, but now walks vigorously three times a week. She takes pride in her condition, shape, and even her age.

> I don't think of myself as old. Seventy-five used to sound old, but I don't think of myself as seventy-five. And I don't much like the term elder. I'm a Super Senior tennis player. I can identify with that. My hair used to be dark and curly; then I colored it every color. After my mother died, I said,

stop pretending. I'm comfortable with my white hair. I also used to be into fashions. I've left that behind. Now I do contrasts with white hair, black frames, and bright colored sweaters. This seems like the right image for me now. My tennis friends, like me, don't think of themselves as old. This is the best time for me, but life has been good. I wouldn't give up one year of my life for anything. I hope I have years yet to live—I'll live to ninety-five, maybe longer.

Relishing her passions for life, art, and tennis, enjoying her family and friends, making a home, and contributing to the community will keep her going for a long time.

Without being conscious of the term, Rebecca has been developing a robust third age life portfolio. Although she has simplified her life since working as a merchandising manager, her passions run in many directions: marriage, home, family, art and an evolving career as painter, tennis, friends, community, a healthy lifestyle, learning, new adventures, and shaping a third age identity as a creative person. Her portfolio keeps changing.

Checking in with her a year later, she reports that she has dropped out of the tennis league to concentrate on her artwork. In the past year she has shown small works of art in San Francisco exhibits, including at city hall, the library, and the Art Institute. She has also been producing large canvasses: "I've been doing a lot of painting this year." And she has done much more showing. She's been playing tennis a couple of times a week with her husband. In the past few years she has added another cherished role: grandmother. Her daughter lives nearby with three children, and her youngest son, also married, has a one-year-old son. Proud of her four grandchildren, she displays their pictures among her artworks, and she and her husband include them as often as possible in family meals at home.

A spiritual dimension courses through her third age life portfolio. A convert to Judaism, she observes traditional holidays, but it is spirituality rather than religion that is important to her.

> I've always been spiritual. I'm not comfortable with organized religion. I converted to Judaism. I feel close to the tradition—I'm connected with the values and spiritual sense I had growing up. I became more spiritual when I went through a mourning period for my son. In Mexico I felt a spiritual connection with the dead through graveyard rituals and powerful female symbols. As I've said, my art is also an expression of my spirituality. Spirit and passion—they infuse my life more than ever.

In building a creative, complex life, Rebecca has been blending together her passions, talents, interests, and loves into a satisfying whole. Her continually unfolding life is saturated, she suggests, with a richness that transcends any conventional sense of retirement. That's success for her now. Her life is also blessed with serendipity, in part because she has persisted in being so engaged, so open to the unexpected, and so resilient.

Mike: *I had gone the whole nine yards: fancy cars, big homes, and expensive vacations; it was not satisfying at all.*

For the past several years Mike has been leading a double life, and loving every bit of it. At fifty-nine he has gotten to where he is today partly by planning and partly by accident. In one life he consults on master planned communities, focusing on leading-edge concepts for building retirement communities for Boomers; in the other life he paints and runs a studio gallery in the Southwest. Mike is still not sure how he got to where he is today, but he is grateful for how his life has been evolving.

When Mike was twelve, his family relocated from southern California, where he had been born and raised, to a rural community in Texas. He didn't like the move one bit. He says he recalls feeling like he had landed on "the dark side of the moon. The white kids didn't mix with the black kids. 'Whites only' drinking fountains were everywhere. I think I was in shock for the first year." He found himself agitated by the change, but he learned to cope. Ironically, almost forty years later Mike would change course on his own; as he did so, he recollected how he had been able to get through that major change as a boy.

After receiving an associate's degree in engineering, Mike got a bachelor's degree in landscape architecture and then a master's degree in urban planning. He taught landscape architecture and urban planning for almost five years at a university in Texas: "Teaching taught me more than I learned, but university politics drove me out; it was intensely political." In the early 1980s he decided to leave teaching and start a business with three partners, specializing in designing master planned communities. The business grew to forty employees. After leading this successful community planning business for almost fifteen years, Mike's world—at age fifty—changed again, dramatically.

> I realized that something was wrong, but I wasn't sure of what it was, or what I had to do next. I had grown tired of chasing the almighty dollar. It seemed that nothing I was doing was ever providing happiness. I had grown tired of living the life I was living. I had gone the whole nine yards: fancy cars, big homes, and expensive vacations; it was not satisfying at all. I did a lot of self-examination, and that self-examination led to a series of insights. The

process was like peeling an onion. Bottom line, I wasn't getting what I wanted. What I realized I wanted can be best described as inner peace.

Mike started to rethink how he had been living, and made changes. First, he downsized material possessions. He separated from, and then divorced his wife of thirty years. About the time of the divorce, Mike's father died, and within a matter of months his mother had heart bypass surgery. Mike felt like he had jumped onto a rocket sled of change. Deciding to move ahead, nevertheless, he set off on a mission "to find inner peace in a damn big hurry." He met Andrew, who after having built a successful insurance business had gone back to school to become a forensic psychologist, and was still active in this role in his seventies. In Andrew, Mike found a mentor and role model.

Andrew was living the kind of life that Mike felt would provide him the inner peace for which he was searching. In addition to practicing forensic psychology in his midseventies, Andrew reads widely and enjoys building elaborate Japanese gardens. Mike relishes Andrew's selfless perspective. Once when Mike confessed to Andrew that he was worried about money, Andrew replied, "Whenever I become fearful about money, I get out my checkbook and write a check to my favorite charity." Mike adopted the same practice; doing so gives him a great sense of release and relief.

Mike embarked on a personalized spiritual journey. Raised in a strict Protestant family, he had walked away from organized religion.

I realized that you don't need organized religion to be a spiritual person. In some ways organized religion is the greatest marketing concept of all time; holy people seem to be continually trying to differentiate the market. My experience has been that too often organized religion causes us to reflect more on our differences than on our similarities. Believe, they preach, but believe our way, or you're on the highway to you know where.

He knew that his own spiritual path was not going to be so well defined: "There were no neon signs marking the way." He started to read books to expand his perspective, including Stephen Hawking's A Brief History of Time, Fred Wolf's Taking the Quantum Leap: The New Physics for Nonscientists, and James Gleick's Chaos: Making a New Science. And he listened to many tapes. How did his perspective change?

> Eventually, I realized that I did not have to judge every-body I saw. I mean, judging people is hard work, right? There's always so much wrong with everyone else. I found it a relief to give up all that stuff. I realized that when I was judging others, I was judging myself. I was beating the dickens out of myself. I was tired of it, and it hurt.

Rather than judging, Mike feels that his perspective is more open and inclusive. He is now looking for lessons—"looking for lessons is a helpful process" to support his journey.

Mike decided to get back into art, because painting had always provided him with great satisfaction: "I had forgotten just how much I missed my art." While still working for the firm, he decided that he wanted to spend considerably more time painting. So he asked his partners for the opportunity to "retire incrementally," suggesting a 20 percent a year reduction in time and pay over four years. He had come to feel a heavy burden as a partner in the firm, because he brought in 90 percent of the work. When times got tough, everyone in the firm came to him, asking, "What are you going to do?" Differences with other partners had been growing. It was time to give more attention to his art. The partners did not know how to handle Mike's proposal to retire incrementally. So they asked him to leave the firm. What a surprise! Mike was overjoyed. The other partners could not understand why Mike was delighted to leave the firm that had taken twenty years to build. Mike's response to this: "They just had no idea."

After leaving, Mike knocked around for six months and then opened a studio gallery. His original intent was to use the gallery to display his own paintings, but local artists came in and asked him to show their works as well. After six months, so many local artists had asked to have their work displayed that he had to expand the gallery. The gallery has not been all that rewarding in financial terms, but it has enabled him to make many new friends in his community. Later, with a couple of former colleagues, he enlarged his work portfolio by starting a consultancy in master planned communities, with a special interest in designing communities for Baby Boomers. But Mike continues to spend most of his time and energy on painting and on his gallery: "It's where I want to be." He enjoys consulting now, because he is doing it with people whom he likes and respects. Talking over his new direction with his friend and mentor Andrew, Mike commented, "I spent fifty years doing the wrong damn things," to which Andrew replied, "It was all part of what you needed to do."

During his first fifty years, Mike dealt with obstacles by "pulverizing them." Obstacles caused him to be frantic. Now, he feels more at peace and is comfortable to let "the universe unfold its plan. It's important to look always for lessons. Ultimately, everything works out for the best." His second marriage reinforces his optimistic belief. His most important relationship now is his new wife Cindy, whom he views as an inspiration. They had been seeing each other for about four years when he asked her to marry him. She had been through a tough time with breast cancer, going for radiation therapy for five weeks at six thirty in the morning. According to Mike, "She did not let her trauma spill over into the rest of her life." Six months after they got married, she was diagnosed with breast cancer in the other breast, and she had to repeat the process of radiation therapy. She has turned this experience into a value-adding enterprise. A former cosmetics artist at a major department store, Cindy has opened her own studio and started a business in permanent cosmetics to help women who have undergone breast surgery and kids with disfigurements. Both husband and wife have become social entrepreneurs.

Mike continues to experience other serendipities in his life. His relationship with his son, who works with Mike's first wife in the field of home healthcare, has changed from that of parent-child to that of a mentor. Mike is eager to share with his son the lessons he has been learning over the last ten years, especially since his son has also grown disenchanted with chasing success: "My son got to see firsthand what long hours did for me, that is, nothing." Now he advises his son, "Look for your happiness." At this point in his life, family and friends have become much more important to Mike. He now goes out of his way to stay in touch. Many of his current friends started off as clients of his consulting practice. With a lifestyle filled with creative stuff and people he loves, he looks forward to shaping emerging third age careers where success will be measured in terms of his social contribution.

> I won't ever retire completely from consulting. I want to design innovative communities for third agers, places where people can live in a genuine community. Right now, builders are confused about what kinds of communities Baby Boomers will want in their third and fourth ages. I see a tremendous opportunity to have an impact on the lives of millions of people. That thought jazzes me up.

Mike admits that he does not take good enough care of himself physically, but spiritual growth is still a priority. He continues to read a lot, particularly books that defy logic and Newtonian concepts of the universe. He wants to grow in his painting and works hard to make his gallery successful. And he will continue consulting on master planned communities. He's optimistic about the future and feels that his new perspective on life is growing stronger as is his love for life: "I'm having the best time of my life. I wouldn't give up what I've gained to go back and do it over, or change anything."

FOUR LESSONS FROM
SERENDIPITOUS THIRD AGERS

AT FIRST BLUSH THE NOTION that we can find patterns in serendipity might seem like one of those ever-dreaded logical contradictions about which we were dutifully warned by philosophy professors, those uptight watchdogs of pure reason. Beware of circular arguments, straw man fallacies, and flawed syllogisms like: all dogs have four legs—and all cats have four legs—therefore, all cats are dogs. Or, is it, all dogs are cats? But teasing out patterns in serendipity is only another form of paradox.

Metaphorically, the four people who have shared their serendipitous third age journeys in this chapter have all been *quilters*. Each has taken the life patches made available and stitched together often-dissimilar shapes, textures, and colors into a majestic mosaic. These third agers have not only accepted serendipity as a present influence in their lives, but they've also embraced it as an energizing force for second growth. How they came to integrate the change in course that comes from planning with the redirection that comes from surprises offers practical lessons for all third agers.

Dig Deep

If the four storytellers in this chapter teach us anything, it is that making a creative transition from the second age into a redefined third age requires a painstaking self-examination. Often fearfully at first, each of these four people was willing to hold up a mirror, stare into it long and hard, and risk the agony of imagining a future that is closer to an authentic ideal.

Eva's mindful reflection while recovering from her fall sparked her creativity and led her to rediscover the resilient girl she had been in Berlin. When Woody was forced from his executive position, he took the time to define his dream job, leading him to a long-term relationship with New York Outward Bound, and then again to design his life as a social entrepreneur. The connection that Rebecca felt at the Day of the Dead celebration in Mexico opened up a way for her to work through her grief at her son's death. Dissatisfied with having gone "the whole nine yards," Mike embarked on a methodical process of self-examination that led him to a series of insights. Remember how he described the process: "like peeling an onion."

Don't kid yourself: taking an intense look inside demands imagination, commitment, courage, and tenacity. Digging deep will require a combination of stubborn self-honesty, ongoing patience with yourself, and disciplined exploration of aspects of yourself that you may have been avoiding, perhaps for a long, long time. Find the passion that makes your soul sing.

Consider a Guide

Digging deep is hard work, and being willing to accept what you find way down there might be unsettling or painful, even terrifying. Consequently, you may choose not to try it alone.

A corollary lesson to digging deep is to consider finding another person, or other people, in whom you trust to mentor, guide, and inspire you on your journey to a redefined retirement. *"Oppresso di stupore, a la mia guida mi volsi,"* Dante confesses in *Paradiso*, "Dazed by bewilderment, to my guide I turned." See, ladies, there's a guy willing to ask for directions. Eva "talked with everyone" she could, partnered with a former student to stage their *covered with ashes* psychodrama, and still goes on retreats in spiritual communities. Rebecca found a gifted grief counselor with whom she worked for over a year to help her deal with her son's death. Later she enlisted friends to enact a living art form as a way of remembering her son. She continues to see a therapist to process her feelings and thoughts. Mike relies on Andrew as a mentor, because Andrew is living the kind of life that Mike feels will provide him the inner peace for which he has been searching. His wife Cindy's courage in triumphing over breast cancer also serves as an inspiration to him.

Underestimating the difficulty of genuine, prolonged self-examination would be foolhardy. If you sense that you will need help when you hold up the mirror to yourself, get it.

REFASHION YOUR IDENTITY

Refashioning your identity is the cornerstone for building new meaning for your third age and retirement. For millennia, philosophers, researchers, and other learned wizards with alphabet soups of credentials strung out behind their names have pondered, dissected, and studied the human phenomenon that goes by *identity*. Whatever strolling academics have had to say, whatever bench scientists have seen through their microscopes, and whatever great minds have published and pronounced, each of us has a role, a responsibility, in shaping her or his own personal identity. We like the metaphor of an orchestra as a way to describe the diverse aspects of a person's identity. We all have multiple talents and melodies within us that need to be integrated into the performance of our lives. In *Multimind*, Robert Ornstein articulates a similar view: "There is no single mind but many; we are a *coalition* [our emphasis], not a single person."

Eva's third age identity is comprised of a mix of her interests: different kinds of work in two countries; ample time for learning; play and creativity; building stronger relationships with her husband, family, and friends; contributing to the community; developing a closer relationship with nature; and taking care of herself. Woody's redefined retirement includes consulting in healthcare labor relations, volunteering with Outward Bound, becoming a social entrepreneur, traveling with his wife, visiting grandchildren, scuba diving, and working out at the YMCA. Recall Rebecca's summation: "We're both passionate about our identities. Mine has been focused on becoming more creative. My husband has been passionate about becoming creative in his own way." Her other passions run in many directions simultaneously, including home, family, tennis, friends, community, a healthy and spiritual lifestyle, learning, and new adventures. Mike paints, runs a studio gallery, consults on master planned communities, reads widely on spiritual topics, and relishes relationships with family and friends. He finds inspiration in his wife's courage, his mentor's wisdom, and his son's forthrightness.

As illustrated by the stirring examples of these four third agers, reshaping your identity will require that you reposition or retune or replace many of the instruments in your orchestra. No single psychological makeover is going to do the trick. You will redefine the person you can become by building a third age life portfolio. You've got work to do, and play to do, and connecting and re-connecting to do, and healing to do, and leading beyond the walls to do, and creating to do. Get off your backside, and get a-goin. Orchestra—portfolio—mosaic—quilt: find the metaphor that works for you. Get in re-shape for your third age and retirement, however you choose to redefine it.

EXPECT—AND ACCEPT—THE UNEXPECTED

Each of the four people in this chapter has received her or his share of third age surprises, both good news and dreadful news, and each has learned to embrace those surprises, even to transform them into springboards for propelling second growth. They offer courageous examples that would humble many of us, for they have in some instances triumphed over obstacles that many of us, reading at a distance, might find insurmountable. They did not allow gut-wrenching losses to drive them to hopelessness.

Eva's fall and battle with chronic pain forced her to slow down and presented her with a windfall of time during which she was able to give mindful reflection to how she might change course. As she observed, "It taught me to rediscover myself." A business recession, a pink slip, and a golden parachute led Woody to his fulltime involvement with Outward Bound. A financial crisis at that organization gave him the opportunity to reshape his relationship with it, resulting in more time to build connections with his family, especially his grandchildren. In mourning the death of her son, Rebecca participated in a Day of the Dead ceremony in Mexico, leading her to a profound appreciation of the connection of the dead with our lives. Further, she moved to a deeper level as she expressed her spirituality through her art. Mike's unexpected separation from his firm provided him the opportunity to paint more regularly and to expand his studio gallery. His new, serendipitous third age careers as a painter, an art impresario, and a consultant on communities for Baby Boomers give him outlets for a trio of passions and affords him the time he wants to spend with family and friends.

Rather than allowing surprises to get the better of them, these third agers have found ways to exploit the unexpected as pathways to greater self-understanding, as fuel for self-growth and greater gratitude, as a reminder of the fragility of cherished relationships, and as a means of moving closer to the reality they most truly desire. They have welcomed their surprises, not shunned them.

CHAPTER SIX

STILL WORKING
AFTER ALL THESE YEARS

And thus, without a Wing
Or service of a Keel
Our Summer made her light escape
Into the Beautiful.

—DICKINSON, "As imperceptibly as grief"

SNAPSHOTS

NOT EVERYONE TAKES RETIREMENT when earned, or offered, not even when there's a ton of money up for the taking. Rupert Murdoch, one of the world's richest, has stated that he'll never retire; the only way he will leave his position is when they carry him out. People with much less money than Murdoch have told us the same thing. Ostensibly, they have become wedded to their jobs—"until death do us part." Faye, whose story we tell later in this chapter, recounted for us how her father's last concern on his deathbed was a deal he was working for an important customer. Many people who can control when they retire are working years past retirement age. In 2003 the *New York Times* published a list of retirement eligible executives who have stayed at the helm, including people like Ernest Gallo, at ninety-three chair of his winery, Leona Helmsley, at eighty-four CEO of Helmsley Enterprises, and William Hilton, filling the chair of Hilton Hotels at seventy-five.

You don't have to be a high-falutin executive to stay at it. Creative artists have often kept working until late in life, like Picasso still painting at ninety-two and Georgia O'Keefe at a hundred. Stanley Kunitz was poet laureate of the United States at ninety-five and spoke publicly and wrote poetry until he died at a hundred. Public leaders sometimes keep working longer than many of their contemporaries. Strom Thurmond kept his Senate seat until he reached a hundred. Claude Pepper, active in Congress well into his eighties, once said, "Life is like riding a bicycle. You don't fall off unless you stop pedaling." Millions over seventy are still pedaling. In the past few years newspaper articles have reported about so many people in their nineties and even over a hundred who bypass retirement and remain employed fulltime that we have stopped clipping.

As people stay healthy and live longer, working way past retirement age will undoubtedly become a trend, especially since retirement savings have started shrinking and mandatory retirement rules are falling by the wayside. Myths about inevitable deleterious effects of aging are beginning to collapse as older people show that they can be more rather than less creative, more rather than less capable, more rather than less savvy. Many people in their sixties and seventies have been developing passions and skills not previously tapped, leading them into totally new careers. Others have had a chance to develop careers in new ways. Jack McKeon, retired from baseball in his sixties, got the chance to reenter the workforce by becoming the manager of the Florida Marlins. Confounding critics, who were appalled by his "old man's" philosophy that the game should be played for fun, at seventy-three he led his players to a World Series championship. Winning can be fun. Clint Eastwood directed, produced, and wrote music for his award winning movie *Mystic River*, demonstrating that at seventy-three he was reaching the peak of his career. Since then he's directed more top films. These people know what fires their souls; after passing seventy they've turned up the heat. Similarly people in this study have changed course to sustain growth and keep working through the third age. What can we learn from them?

We have suggested that work can continue to play a significant role in any plan for a vital and purposeful second half of life. However, work defined within a second age context can act as a barrier rather than as an avenue to growth after fifty. A consultant to family enterprises told us that founders of a business often refuse to let go. As an example he reported a session with executives in a small company that needed new direction. The founder would not pass the reins to his son. Exasperated, the son, the president, said to the ninety-three-year-old father, "If you insist on running this business your way, you're welcome to it. I'm sixty-five and I'm retiring."

A basic requirement for successful transition into a fulfilling third age is learning to let go, to become free of past commitments in order to explore new opportunities. It is hard to let go if you haven't first done the hard internal work of visualizing what is most important, what you want, and where your passion lies in the next part of the journey. Without mindful reflection, we can easily become stalled. Holding on is looking back. As the baseball sage Satchell Paige once advocated, "Don't look back. Something might be gaining on you."

One accomplished woman revealed she was having a hard time with retirement because she missed the excitement and challenge she had found in work. Ellen had enjoyed careers as a teacher, administrator, flight attendant, professor of communication, and executive coach. This last career provided her with challenge, satisfaction, and a substantial income. As her client base declined, she gradually slipped into retirement. At seventy she misses her work:

> I'm an upbeat person, but there's something wrong. A friend said I'm thrashing about like a man who feels lost in retirement. I'm involved in programs and on boards, but there's something missing. If you're not earning, is your work valuable? I don't think so. Work was everything for me. Without it I feel like I'm lost, without direction. Work was my focus; I don't have one now. My work used every part of me—my intelligence, problem solving ability, caring about people, intuition. It's who I am. A couple of weeks ago I spent time working with a bright executive who couldn't communicate. After several sessions, he was transformed. He spoke like he never had before. I left the last session feeling higher than if I were on top of a mountain. I miss my work. I haven't yet found a passion outside it.

Ellen was searching for a way of life that would provide her with rewards equivalent to those she formerly had found in work, particularly those in her last career. She admitted that she had felt inhibited not only from letting go but also from releasing her imagination to find another passion to express. The core of growth involves discovering the person you want to become and redefining your work to express an important part of your personal vision. Ellen apparently hadn't yet tapped that core. Many people don't. They freeze a view of themselves and their work within a second age framework.

In deciding on whether or not to retire, each of us needs to consider what work means personally and learn to redefine it to suit the way we want to live. As one man told us, "My job is not my work." Like more and more people who are finding a second or third act in their working lives, John at seventy-five is vital and fully employed in his own enterprise. A fan of *The Third Age*, he has written us about his experience of growth and renewal: "I have constantly been redefining my work. As a consultant with my own business, I find great satisfaction acting as coach and mentor to senior executives and young graduates. My work also includes active participation in civic, fraternal, and educational activities."

John is still working nearly fulltime in the business he founded forty years ago. His work, redefined, has led him into a third age career, a concept we explore more fully below and throughout this chapter. John has also been developing a third age life portfolio that adds complexity and balance to his life. A top priority in the portfolio is his family and marriage to his wife of forty-six years. He has also become committed to a healthy lifestyle and remains physically active, walking and swimming on a regular basis. He reads voraciously: history, business, quality fiction, and current events. Habitually, he starts with a daily plan to reward himself, offer service to others, and enrich his life. "The key," he writes, "is to create events that are exciting, fulfilling, and sustain growth both intellectually and emotionally."

THIRD AGE CAREERS

THIRD AGE CAREERS OFTEN FORM A KEY COMPONENT of a third age life portfolio. The transition from second age to third age requires that people and organizations break comfortable links with each other. Individuals can create entirely new kinds of interconnections with organizations. One way to make new, more flexible connections will be for organizations to encourage individuals to shape third age careers. *Careers* is not a typo: we see the third age as a time of multiple reinvented careers, sometimes emerging simultaneously. Some authors have written about the role of a third age career for retirees, but often as a way to extend a second age career.

We do not mean by third age careers simply jumping second age career tracks, or changing disciplines, or down stepping from a management position back to the technical ladder. Neither do we intend for the idea to encompass busywork jobs, volunteer or for pay, that some third agers take to keep from getting bored. Our notion of third age careers is that third agers can revitalize themselves, the organizations with which they choose to be associated, and their communities by creating a flexible, often shifting work portfolio, a kind of ensemble of careers. Each work endeavor might not be necessarily logically linked to other ventures in the mix. For individuals to create such a potpourri of careers while still involved in an organization will require formal organizations to embrace them, support (including funding) them, and benefit from them. The key is that any and all activities that are part of third age careers tap into the many dimensions of a person's creativity.

Individuals, professions, and organizations must reexamine how they have come to think of a career. As with many concepts integral to the second age, a career is most commonly thought of as a linear progression. The term suggests rushing ahead, or at least wanting to rush ahead. We speak of a person as climbing the career ladder. Starting at the bottom is considered in conventional wisdom to be a good place to begin. You've got to work your way UP. Career pathing was all the rage in the 1980s. Many companies have job families called "professional ladders." An Engineer I becomes an Engineer II, an Engineer III, and so on. Fast-rising stars are given special assignments to prepare them for more responsibility down the road. These hot shots are said to be "on the fast track." Should they stumble, they are spoken of as having "derailed." Soldiers, sailors, airmen, and marines aspire to be promoted to the next highest rank. Certain civil service employees see their pay go up by way of a step increase. Ladders, tracks, ranks, steps. In the second age a career is all about getting in line, about getting somewhere else, somewhere down the line. We are not suggesting that cultivating professional, technical, and managerial talent is *not* a step-by-step process. Of course it is. But in the third age, sequential, step-by-step advancement must be displaced by simultaneous, multidimensional growth driven by creativity. Ladders, tracks, ranks, and steps must give way to hubs and spokes, to webs, to starbursts.

ORGANIZATIONAL SUPPORT FOR THIRD AGE CAREERS

Institutional support is crucial for third age careers. In this book we mainly focus on how individuals might take a creative look at retirement, and find imaginative ways to redefine it. From the six paradoxical principles of growth and renewal and the individual life stories we are sharing, one thing emerges as unquestionable: redefining retirement is a profoundly personal journey, an individual endeavor both frightening and exciting, and for each of us that journey can take many paths. Our proposition has been that igniting individual creativity empowers second growth, making it possible for a person's life after fifty to be a time of enormous personal expansion and reinvigorating interpersonal connections, a time of fulfillment. So if we are in the main talking about personal prospects for the second half of life, how do organizations fit in? During the second age many of us were, perhaps still are, connected to one or more formal organizations. Take, for example, the authors of this book. Bill has been connected with universities and colleges, as a teacher, as an administrator, and as a leader. Jim has been employed by a fast-food company, a university, the U.S. Army, a federal agency, an international corporation, a consulting firm, and the clients of his consulting and coaching practices. Both have become entrepreneurs in a new organization, The Center for Third Age Leadership.

Even professionals whom we might not at first glance associate with formal organizations, such as physicians, attorneys, or CPAs with their own practices, have close personal and economic ties to formal organizations: physicians partner with pharmaceutical companies, laboratories, and hospitals; attorneys collaborate with clients, government agencies, and court systems; and CPAs work with clients, tax agencies, and nonprofit organizations. If hospitals run short of nurses or get into financial trouble, the healing effectiveness, and income, of its partner physicians are threatened. If a court system becomes backlogged and dysfunctional, the legal effectiveness, and fees, of attorneys are at risk. If client companies get into financial trouble, a CPA's livelihood is in peril.

In the second age most of us gave to and took from—perhaps still give to and take from—formal organizations. Are third agers better off with organizations or without them? And, are organizations better off with or without third agers? Until now, both individuals and organizations put a check in the "without" box. That view is beginning to change.

The connections with professions, organizations, and institutions can continue to the mutual benefit of both third agers and organizations. But the relationship has to change, on the part of both parties. Third age careers can form a key component of a third age life portfolio. However, if organizations are not willing to reexamine how they think of a career, and—more important—if they are not willing to partner with employees in re-shaping what careers can look like for third agers, individuals will abandon the organizations they have served for many years. Third age careers are made possible if, and only if, professions and companies collaborate with individuals to redefine what is meant by a career.

A smooth transition from second age to–do-ism to third age fulfillment requires that both people and organizations break long-standing links with each other and create new kinds of interconnections. The old connections will not survive the change. We must let go of them to shape new forms of employment agreements. Our proposition is that third agers can use third age careers to revitalize both themselves and the formal organizations and institutions with which they choose to be associated. For individuals to create a mixture of careers will require formal organizations to embrace them, support (including funding) them, and benefit from them.

Later in this chapter you will read about Dan, whose company felt that it could not afford to let him retire early, and so they allowed him to reshape his career in a manner that benefited both himself and the organization. Had the executive leaders of the company not been willing to accommodate Dan's interests, he would have certainly checked out by now, leaving the enterprise with a huge competency hole at a time the marketplace was in turmoil. Ted, whom you'll meet in chapter 7, has been designing an unprecedented third age career in his architectural firm only because the partners have been willing to create a new personal compact for his tenure. Woody forged a new version of his third age career because the administration of Outward Bound realized they had too good a thing to ignore and so worked out an arrangement that satisfies everyone involved.

One key in developing third age careers is to tap into the many dimensions of a person's creativity. But another key lies in an organization's willingness to experiment with new employment models. As a third ager works to frame his or her third age careers, he or she will abandon existing organizational allegiances and make a different kind of commitment, a creativity commitment. We do not know exactly how this idea will blossom. We do know that if the stakeholders in formal organizations partner in imaginative ways with their own, and other third agers, third age careers will burst forth as a booming force in the workplace, a kind of turbo drive boosting the horsepower of our National economic engine and radically changing the common notion of retirement. Not a Boomer bust, but rather a Boomer boom.

Organization stewards must take the lead in redefining both careers and retirement from the perspective of the organization's future. Stewards include anyone accountable for the continuity and survivability of an organization, what might be termed the organization's *continuity infrastructure*. Board members, C-level officers, and other members of a senior leadership team are all easy calls for this group. Stewards also include strategic planners, Human Resources generalists, financial analysts, workforce planners, chief technical specialists, labor relations administrators, attorneys, and so on.

Any organization that does not figure out how to support third age careers for key people of retirement age will find its continuity infrastructure under siege. Organization stewards must recognize and acknowledge that their enterprise is facing new kinds of business risks, especially because of changing demographics that threaten organizational survivability in a way not seen before in our lifetimes. You know the mind-numbing numbers. Now is the time for leaders to learn what new threats are on the horizon. The bottom line? From a strategic staffing point of view, third agers comprise an enormous reservoir of untapped, underutilized human assets, a ready reserve of talent, experience, and leadership. Which organizations, professions, and communities will have enough foresight to embrace and encourage third age careers? They'll be the marketplace winners in the next three decades.

The people in this chapter have been building third age careers as they develop new acts in their working lives. They have been learning to unlock old perspectives; they keep growing by redefining themselves and their life work beyond the bounds of a job. You might want to follow them. Abandon the conceptions of work you developed during your second age. Build a new framework for work after fifty, a framework based on your vision of what you want in the next stage of your life. If you continue to judge your work in your third age by the norms of your second age world of work, you risk subjecting yourself to great frustration, disappointment, and even self-resentment. Let go of second age criteria. Find your own third age center and build your work around it. As you grow older the center will continue to move. Move with it. Change your work to accommodate it.

Dan: *For the first time in my career, I determined not to orchestrate my future proactively. I decided to pull the plug and see what came my way.*

Dan at sixty-two began pursuing what he labels as a "post-career career." After thirty-five years in the insurance business, Dan decided that he needed a change, but he did not know exactly how to go about making the change he felt he needed. As do many people contemplating a major life transition, Dan began by reading widely on retirement. Moreover, he started working with a life coach to help with self-reflection and analysis. Many of the books Dan read proposed that people begin the process of transitioning into retirement by building a retirement plan. Dan, however, fully committed to his company and to his field sales force, simply did not have the time to make such a plan: "I was living a totally absorbing life with my work. I was so absorbed in what I was doing day to day that I literally did not have any time left over to kick back, reflect, and think about where I was going and the steps I needed to take to get there. I resolved that I simply had to stop and let the future come to me."

Dan chose to unplug without a transition plan: "I decided simply to let go and see what came my way." He walked into company headquarters and announced that he would be retiring in two years at age sixty-two, period. They were in shock.

A graduate of an Ivy League university, Dan had always been interested in leadership, particularly field leadership in sales. He had climbed the ladder at his company, spending the requisite term at corporate headquarters and receiving many rapid promotions over his career. In 1980 after professing a desire "to get turned loose in the market," Dan was transferred to a major metropolitan area to revive "a beat up sales operation." His hard-hitting, innovative efforts at redeveloping the regional market and growing the business turned out to be so successful that retirement became financially feasible for him sooner than he had anticipated. After twenty years in redeveloping that regional market, Dan determined that it was time "to back away from it all, not knowing what might come next." Dan was not yet sure of what he wanted, but he had seen in depressing terms what he did not want.

I have two friends who have turned in their retirement
paper. One friend is vibrant and excited about retirement.
The other is retiring at the end of the year and has no
idea at all what he is going to be doing when he wakes up
on New Years Day. He is already depressed, already sitting around acting like he's waiting to die. I resolved that
I was not going to be like that. I am not going to check
out and wait around in the lobby for the grim reaper's taxi
to pull up front and call my name.

For the first few weeks after giving notice that he intended to retire in two years, Dan did "absolutely nothing." With
his family's blessing he took off with riding buddies on a ten-
day bicycle tour in Europe.

I did not know what was going to come next, but I knew
that clearing my head was going to be crucial for ensuring
that I remained open to the future. My fear was that the
muddle in my head would keep me from seeing the future
clearly. I had to empty my head of all the clutter that had
used to seem so important but that now no longer
seemed as significant as it once did. After I returned from
the cycling trip, I continued to do nothing for a few more
months. I had to let my "must do muscles" heal; I had to
let my "can do muscles" strengthen.

Within three months the company came calling, anxious
to retain Dan's talent and leadership in field sales. Together
with executive leaders at the highest levels of the company,
Dan formulated a new role for himself for the next four years.
The company's leaders had recognized that the business climate was changing rapidly and that the company had to
morph from a one-product insurance company selling mainly to white males to a financial security firm selling a broad

range of financial products to an increasingly diverse client base throughout the country. But the company's leaders simply did not know how to go about making the change tactically. That's what they recognized they needed Dan to do. As a senior vice president confessed to him, "There's a lot going on in the marketplace that we don't understand, and we could sure use your help in figuring it all out." The company was offering Dan a third age career, or what he calls his post-career career. This third age career gave him a chance to reconceptualize his work to better suit how he wanted to live and evolve in his sixties.

Dan liked the idea of acting as an internal change agent to transform the company to which he had committed thirty-five years; he was excited by the challenge.

> I thought about it, looked at the organization structure, considered our second home, and concluded, "I've got to do this." I'm so excited about what I'm doing now. I feel like I've been re-invented, re-potted, re-born. Every day I go to work I can't wait to get in there and get at it. I made a four-year commitment to the company. After this I'll do something else, but I imagine I'll keep on working 40–50 percent of the time.

Dan commutes by flying back and forth from his home city to corporate headquarters on a regular basis, occasionally accompanied by his wife, an attorney who specializes in estate planning. Initially, a few executives were skeptical about his proposal to reshape his relationship with the company and to create an ideal job for himself. The corporate mentality has not yet caught up with third age possibilities. Dan told us that he did have champions who realized that it was critical for the company to have a grasp of what was happening in the marketplace. They understood that Dan's principal strength was an up-to-date, on-the-ground insight into what changes were occurring there. Gradually, the skeptics came to appreciate what he was contributing. "Wow, this could be helpful." Dan recounted the following vignette as evidence of his emerging impact on the future direction of the company.

> I feel great because I'm in position to deliver bad news in a way that is helpful to the company. Just yesterday I had lunch with the CEO and let him know straightforwardly, without any sugar coating, why the latest pet project of a high-level executive would result in a disaster in the marketplace. Lunch with the CEO. You cannot get any better access to the business. You know, I'm not running for re-election, and so I can quite forthrightly, and tactfully, speak my mind regarding what I feel is in the best interest of the company. I can tell it like it is without fear of being put in the corporate penalty box. Think about that. I'm an "untouchable." Now, that's invigorating!

Dan has expressed a desire to continue to grow, to continue to make a difference. Since boyhood he has always believed in the YMCA triangle of body, mind, and spirit. While changing the shape of his work, he has been designing a more complex, better-balanced life. He continues to cycle avidly, reads widely, and has a strong belief in a greater being: "I believe that we control the input and that God controls the output." As with others, we asked him what makes him happy. What makes Dan's soul sing?

> That's easy. Relationships with people: my wife, my family, my children, and my close friends. My whole career I've gone out of my way to make friends outside the company, for example my college alumni association, homeowners associations, youth athletics, and church. My best friend is six years older than me, and I have friends who are

much younger than me. Being able to connect with people of all ages is important to me: I learn something different from my younger friends than I do from my older friends, and vice versa. I don't see myself as any particular age. I feel that it's vital to have relationships with people of all ages.

Dan has undergone a major shift in perspective since his decision to unplug and let the future come to him. The shift is apparent in his approach to obstacles. In the past, Dan took a fairly head-on approach to dealing with the conflicts he faced both at home and at work. His old competitive tactics resulted in high levels of stress, further compounding his effectiveness in overcoming hurdles. Today, he does not "obsess about setbacks any more." He is now quick to apologize and handles conflicts much more circumstantially that he did formerly. Dan's shift in perspective was in part triggered by something his life coach had told him. Dan had viewed power mainly as "abused not used." The coach suggested to Dan that he appreciate how power can be applied for good and that he learn to use power for good.

Dan will continue to focus on growing in the leadership arena. He has learned to accept who he's become and is willing to step out with that. He is both confident and humble, and he wants to share what he is doing with others, knowing in his heart he is making a big contribution to his company. He feels both proud of that accomplishment and privileged to be helping a values-rooted organization successfully navigate a major transition. In summing up his service, Dan remarked, "I'm helping a hundred-and-fifty-year-old company re-tool itself for the next hundred and fifty years." Any regrets? Dan offered only one, and it turns out to be a paradox.

My only regret about my post-career career is that I didn't do it sooner. I asked myself, "Why did I wait so long?" On the other hand, I was like a coiled spring, which enabled me to get out of the blocks fast. Before unplugging, I most likely would have beat myself up for having waited so long, but I haven't. It would be a waste of time and energy. I'm just looking forward to whatever's next.

In developing a post-career career, Dan exemplifies a possibility you may have. Although some people shift into a different arena, often becoming entrepreneurial in expressing a newly discovered passion, Dan found a new opportunity in the company he had served for over thirty years. His company made an adjustment that supports Dan's growth. In return it benefits from his contributions that otherwise would have lost.

Joan: *I'm doing what I like to do best. I like to build. I get bored when things are too ordinary. There's always something that needs doing here.*

Becoming acquainted with Joan has been like opening a Christmas stocking. A small, attractive, quietly dynamic woman, she's the type who might easily get carded when asking for a senior admission ticket of admission. When learning her age, people inevitably say, "What? She's seventy-five?" Especially in the third age, appearances can be deceiving. Joan is employed, working two different jobs, giving about 150 percent of herself and loving it. She has so far retired three times. She identified with our story of a man who said, "I retired for about a year. But I failed retirement and found other work." Joan may have failed retirement, but she has succeeded in virtually everything else she has tried.

The oldest of three daughters, Joan grew up in a small university town in northern California. She was the first in her family to go to college, which was a major accomplishment to her parents, who didn't finish high school. After completing high school, Joan went to a hospital nursing school and received her RN within two years. She then married Bruce, her high school boyfriend, and started practicing as a nurse and raising a family. After fifty-four years of marriage, they have three sons, a daughter, ten grandchildren, and their first great-grandchild. On their fiftieth wedding anniversary they got remarried in the same church, followed by a big celebration that their children planned for them. Many family members and old friends were on hand, including a circle of her friends from high school, with whom she has remained close.

Joan practiced nursing for sixteen years and decided she wanted something different. At the age of thirty-seven she went to college to attain a BS. Back in the sixties she was the oldest student in the class by far. She was also pregnant with their fourth child. Bruce quit his job to stay home and take care of kids so that she could focus on learning. As Joan was completing her degree, a director of nursing told her to enter graduate school to get an MS so that she could return as a teacher. A year later, degree in hand, she began a new career as an educator, teaching nursing and leadership courses. She rose to the rank of full professor, then became department chair, and eventually Dean of Arts and Sciences in this large state university.

After fifteen years there she qualified for retirement, having acquired an enviable healthcare package and pension. She decided to stay home, but her first retirement didn't last more than a few months. She could have settled into retirement, but didn't really want to. She soon received an offer to become dean at a prestigious private university in San Francisco and took it. After eight years in that position, as the only female administrator in the university, the president asked her to fill a vacancy to become interim vice president of academic affairs. After filling that position for three three years, she would have settled into it, but it required a priest, who was eventually found and installed. So after eleven years as a university leader, she decided she would finally retire for really real. She and Bruce had a home in the hills, where he raised quarter horses, as well as cows, and chickens. There would be plenty to keep her busy at home. She stayed put for several months, but missed people and the challenge of a job.

Quite unexpectedly she got a call from a former colleague who had joined a search firm. She told Joan that there was a college in the Midwest that needed her as president. She and Bruce agreed that it might be an interesting adventure to pull up stakes to experience life in a different setting. She went for an interview and discovered it was a good school, but in tough shape. They asked her to become president, to help get the college back on track. She agreed, but on condition that she could continue her other careers as a book editor and officer of an international nursing society. At sixty, for the first time in her life she had a job she could walk to. Bruce retired as an accountant and took his horses to raise in the Midwest. Their new life became busier for Joan when she became president of the international nursing society at the same time she was college president: "Running around the world from 1993–1995 for the nursing society was a pretty exciting time."

After seven years in the Midwest, with the college restored to good standing, she and her husband were ready to return to California. She then retired for the third time. Actually, it was semiretirement, because Joan continued her third age career as an editor and writer while they settled into a new home in the Bay Area. The move back gave her time needed to catch up on a growing family and her circle of old friends: "I had a lot to do—settling a new home, reconnecting with family, editing and writing—but I missed people." Three years later she got another call, this time from a local university vice president, who asked if she could help out with a quality nursing program that had begun to develop some serious problems. As president of the nursing society Joan had come to know this program and respected its fine qualities. She agreed to help out as a consultant. Within a year she realized this program would not find the right person to bring it back to health, and so she consented to stay on as a department chair. At seventy, why would she do this? "I love picking up messes. This was a challenge I couldn't resist. I couldn't let the program continue to go downhill."

After five years as chair, she says she's more than fulltime. But she doesn't arrive when other administrators do. She has a flexible schedule that allows her to miss rush hour traffic and put in time when and where needed. She often stays on campus into evening hours and is involved often on weekends.

> We have a strong undergraduate degree program, which is
> now linked with a large healthcare system in California.
> Our graduate program has grown. We're developing new
> ventures in several areas. I'm totally involved—teaching
> as well as chairing. I'm doing what I like to do best. I like
> to build. I get bored when things are too ordinary. There's
> always something to do here. This is a growth period for
> me. I'm still learning. I hate grading all those papers—but
> you know, the students are doing all kinds of research,
> and I'm learning so much from them. Right now I'm writ-
> ing with another colleague about how nurses can use
> technology to become more effective. We're exploring the
> nursing shortage and want to change the way nurses
> nurse. In this situation I'm growing all the time—

acquiring knowledge, meeting new people, starting new ventures, building fine programs. It doesn't seem like work. This is doing what I love.

How long will she continue her third age careers as academic leader and editor for the nursing society? Five or ten more years? "Well, probably. Why not? I'm in good health for someone my age. I'd rather continue this and be productive, than stay home." A defining factor in her evolving life has been a commitment to sustained personal growth, rather than giving in to the conventional, decrement model of aging that as a nurse she knows too well. She firmly believes that she is young enough to be highly productive, learn, lead, and contribute to others. As she has redefined her work, Joan has also been transforming the meaning of retirement. It's a word she doesn't like:

> I don't like retirement. I think it's a bad word. I like your idea of the third age better. It suggests potential. Retirement sounds like giving up. I just don't like the implied idea that you're no good anymore, the idea that you're being trashed. Not retirement, we need renewal. I see that we have transitions in life. That's what I'm in. Some things I still do, others I've dropped. But whatever I'm doing, I still want to have a feeling of accomplishment. That's what success means to me now.

Accomplishing, productivity, contributing, and renewal— these terms play prominent roles as she thinks about the quality of her life now. As she reflected about her upcoming seventy-fifth birthday, she commented,

> Do you know that means I've lived three quarters of a century? That's pretty amazing, I think. I believe I might have another quarter. As I get older, I can't imagine not

doing what I like to do. It's important to do what you love. I want to keep doing that. My dad lived to be ninety-six. I took that test on the Internet and found I should live to be at least ninety-two. I don't want to be a hundred if I can't do things or have Alzheimer's. I know a lot about that, and I don't want to end up that way. I'm optimistic about my future—I always have thought good things will come. When things are bad, we can learn from them. Hope is important to me.

Joan has been learning from her three failures in retirement, discovering how to make transitions into new adventures that keep her vital and satisfied. Like others who have so impressed us, she has been finding ways to shape a life that abounds in an experience of flow. One of her secrets has been to clarify and identify those aspects in life most important to her.

When asked to name those aspects, she had a ready response:

Most important is my family. Even though I'm busy with careers, they come first. My husband and I have a good life. We enjoy having fun together, spending a couple of weeks in our timeshare in Kauai and getting away to Napa to discover new wines. We love to take our dog to explore new sites. And we have ten grandchildren to play with—and now a great grandchild. Most of our family lives close by now, but we visit those who live away.

Next in importance is being productive. In addition to my work here, I'm publishing. I'm acquisitions editor for the nursing society. I just finished editing two books. I find the author, define the book, and do the editing. This is my second job. I'm also writing, right now with another person. I also love to garden. I used to do more, as well as knit and

embroider. Not any more. My husband and I used to grow
a lot of things. It's simpler now, but still important.

I'm also taking good care of myself. I eat well, sleep
enough, and walk. I used to exercise more, but I need to
get my knee fixed so that I can start again. And I'm still
growing. My growth is mostly intellectual at this point, but
also spiritual. We've always been active in the Catholic
Church. We enjoy the new parish, which is filled with young
people. We used to teach kids, but not any more. We stay
involved, but I'm not comfortable with all the church's
teaching. It's not the way I was brought up, but being spiritual is not the same as being religious. My growth has a
spiritual side, and it involves learning more about myself.

While still working after all these years, Joan has been
building a third age life portfolio that includes several
careers, a complex family life, time for fun and travel, intellectual and spiritual growth, community involvement, and
self-care. She has been changing course during the past
twenty-five years, navigating with a clear set of priorities, a
sense of adventure, and an optimistic spirit that encourages
her to keep trying something new and different. Within the
rich complexities of her life, what makes her soul sing?

My soul sings when I'm doing something that makes
someone's life better, when good things happen, and
when I'm with people who are happy. I mother everybody—I just can't help it. I don't like to see people
unhappy. I don't want to do things for them. I want to
help them help themselves.

Joan's view of happiness and success resonates with the
new paradigm of leadership: leaders serve others as they
create environments in which followers realize their potential

and become leaders themselves. Like others in our study, she has been thinking hard and deep about the kind of legacy she leaves. Her third age has been a creative period in which to build a legacy that extends to healthcare, education, her family, her community, and the future. How fortunate the world is that in her several attempts to retire, she failed.

Carl: *I'm now starting my fifth career. I have distaste for the term* retirement. *That's what you do when you go to bed; you retire for the night. I'm reinventing myself again. I see my career changes as turning points in my life, as times of new beginnings, not as times of retirement.*

For Carl at sixty-five, each turning point in his life has sent him in a different direction. The first turning point came when he interrupted college studies to join the Marines. Carl came from a large family in Missouri and went off to an Ivy League college, where for the first three years he mainly majored in partying and heavy drinking. Asked to leave, he entered the Marines during the Vietnam War and became a helicopter pilot. During a five-year military career he rose to the rank of captain, served a one-year tour of duty in Vietnam, was awarded the Air Medal seven times and a Navy Commendation Medal, and taught jet pilots to fly helicopters. That experience was "a significant time of maturing, gaining self-esteem, and growing." While in the Marines he met and married Glenda; together they returned to the Ivy League college, where he was welcomed back. Two years later he graduated in the top third of his class.

Carl went to work for an international bank in New York and raced up the corporate ladder. Upon returning from a three-year posting to London, he began to experience an inner current that would send him in a new direction. While participating in a leadership development seminar, Carl began to realize that his values were different from his colleagues at the bank. Instead of providing financial services and managing investment portfolios, he wanted to provide service to the community. Consequently, he took a leadership role in the bank's community relations and public affairs department. In retrospect, he senses that move didn't help advance his career with the bank. He was disappointed when—having served the bank for twenty-five years—a promotion to his boss's position was given to someone else. Partly from disappointment, but mainly from a clear vision of who he wanted to become, he left the bank. He had begun to realize that "the bank's expectation of me and my own expectation of what I wanted to become were in conflict." He decided to be true to himself and took the risk of starting out on his own.

With a retirement package and a "vaguely formed vision to serve in the nonprofit sector," he launched his own consulting company and soon found this new career to be satisfying and financially sustainable. Along the way he discovered the National Executive Service Corps (NESC), a nonprofit organization of retired executives who provide management-consulting services pro bono to other nonprofits. After doing volunteer work with them for five years, Carl was asked to take over the leadership of the regional program. He led this organization for eight years, during which time its operations grew, contacts with state and business organizations developed, and its influence increased. Seeing that he could leave the organization in a healthy state, he sought a successor for this leadership role so that he could pursue another vision.

A driving motivational force in the past twenty-five years has been his religious faith. Carl's family had attended the

Presbyterian Church as he was growing up. He went along, but church never meant much to him. As a young couple with two adopted children, he and his wife began attending a local Presbyterian Church, where they became involved with a group of young parents who had formed an intentional community. Carl and Glenda were deeply impressed by the spiritual depth of this group. One day, feeling stressed and slightly depressed, Carl went into a church to pray and felt for the first time that God was a dynamic presence in his life. This experience was another turning point for him: "Since then I have lived with the conviction that God is real and can be trusted." During the past twenty years prayer, commitment, and service have been very important to him.

> I have wanted to become more involved in expressing my
> spirituality in some way. I guess the main force in my
> journey has been an ever deepening desire to find God's
> will for me in the world and to continue to grow in my
> awareness of the gifts and talents I bring to whatever I
> feel led to undertake. What has been most meaningful
> has been the sense that I was genuinely being of service
> to others. I still derive joy when I get positive feedback
> from people in the community or church school students
> and parents.

In his church he has been an active layman, ruling elder, Sunday school teacher, and choir member. In the larger community he has served on a variety of boards: in healthcare, international grant making and development, nonprofit law, community housing, creative living and aging, and voluntary international action. Carl's faith has been leading him in yet another direction. As he was looking for a successor in NESC, an old friend who had begun a new career in the ministry serving in hospices and hospitals visited Carl and Glenda.

The possibility of following a similar path intrigued him. A chaplain friend invited him to help out in a nearby hospital, where he was touched by the connection he felt with the sick and dying. When he learned of a clinical pastoral education program in a nearby medical center, he decided to enter it. At sixty-five Carl was launching his fifth career as he began this graduate program that includes being a chaplain intern. This experience has both unsettled and reassured him.

> I have been doing time on the floor Thursdays from seven thirty to four. My first time out I was extremely nervous. But after several days I started to become more comfortable approaching people I do not know, and who are in some degree of distress. I try to be helpful. Some situations have been intense, like when I minister to a family with a loved one who is terminally ill. I am learning to listen supportively and am trying to be a healing presence. I recently presented my first verbatim to our trainee group, which turned out to be very emotional for me. I realized that in reporting, my feelings at the time of my mother's death resurfaced. We are learning that situations will often remind us of events from our past. The more at peace we are with our own emotions, the more effective we can be as chaplains.

Carl feels that this experience has opened up a new arena of learning and personal growth. He has explored how to become more formally involved in ministry and has begun the process of becoming a commissioned lay pastor with his local church and Presbytery. He says that he is graduating to a new opportunity. Two years later he put this plan on hold as he assumed a leadership position in both a nonprofit organization and in his Presbyterian Church.

At the core of Carl's new growth is a deepening awareness of who he is and wants to become. For years he has seen himself becoming a more caring and positive person. In his final years at the bank he was known as someone who listens, a person to whom people could go for honest conversations and genuine support. Following his graduation from the bank, he has also discovered a feminine side of his personality developing. As he becomes more open to others, and more nurturing, he has also been taking better care of himself. In his thirties, he started to drink heavily again. In the church group he found support to quit both drinking and smoking. He and his wife have been building a healthy lifestyle; and recently Carl has been going to a health club three times a week, using the treadmill for cardiovascular work and weight machines for upper body strength. His physical fitness was evident during a third age retreat, when he impressively negotiated a demanding ropes course thirty feet above his cheering colleagues.

Most of his adult life has been driven by a search for perfection, to attain an ideal self. Carl is learning, he tells us, to be more comfortable with limiting a search for perfection, to focus on what he is actually able to influence. He feels content with a third age career in which he will get much less visibility and public recognition than he did in the previous four: "In this new career change I will be less visible to the outside world and more engaged in ministering to needy people, in a hospital or nursing home or prison. But what I will be doing will be consistent with who I am, my sense of God's call, and my need to make things better."

While work has always been one of his core values, he has continued to redefine it to fit with his personal evolution. Finding his center, he has been building his work around it. Until now he has been able to balance his need to do good with earning an income sufficient to support his family. But his wife worries about financial uncertainty, especially since his career changes have not been uniformly remunerative and his chaplain's work currently brings in no income. Carl has explored possibilities of becoming an adjunct professor in a business college and is also doing consulting to keep money coming in. A colleague has encouraged him to work with him on a new investment idea. For the past twenty years, particularly the last five, Carl's third age career has been acquiring several different components.

In addition to doing several types of work as part of his third age careers, Carl now allots more time for play. One of his loves is performing music. For the past thirty years he has been playing the guitar and singing, for himself and family, in church, and at special gatherings. Singing makes his soul sing. He also has become an expert bridge player and plays as often as a busy schedule allows. While in the graduate program he is allotting time both to play bridge and to give bridge lessons. Another vital part of his third age life portfolio involves spending time with his wife and two adult children. As he reflects on the complexity of his portfolio life, he tells us, "In many ways, life continues to seem full and rich. I feel blessed."

For the past couple of years Carl has been sharing with us his views on retirement. Like most others in our study, he doesn't like the term or its stereotypical implications. While the bank has classified him as retired, he has instead thought of this time as one of *new beginnings*. He has maintained a philosophy that the end of one thing contains the potential for the beginning of something new. In reflecting about the turning points in his life, he wrote us:

> In looking back, my thinking at the time of beginning
> each new career has always related to the search for
> something new, hopefully better, and usually building on

what went before. I am undertaking this new training in a belief that God is calling me to something beyond what I had been doing. By graduating from the last position, I can make time needed to prepare for that call. I have related to the character of Pippin in the Broadway show. I was engaged in a frustrating search for perfection. In the end he realized, as I have, that you are not truly free if you cannot be tied down to something.

Carl has been redefining retirement with a ensemble of third age paradoxes—ending yet beginning, more committed yet freer, more focused yet more open to change, more serious about work yet more involved in play. His retirement has freed him to start new third age careers and to express his religious faith more fully, his love of people, his need to serve, and his passion for play. *Still working after all these years* provides Carl with more meaning, growth, and fun than could a barrel of conventional retirement programs.

Faye: *I'm going to keep on working for the next five to ten years. Why not? I love what I do. I get to meet new, interesting people all the time. I'm not ready to give that up yet.*

At sixty-one Faye was hitting her stride. A real estate agent in a major metropolitan area, Faye found her way through troubled times in her late thirties and early forties and has since forged a successful career based on considerable talent, moxie, street smarts, and customer service. She has always taken ownership of her own destiny and as a consequence dared to make periodic gut-wrenching decisions that have propelled her forward. For a woman who grew up in the era of *Father Knows Best*, to make such trailblazing decisions, and stick by them, and succeed, has required both personal courage and the encouragement of people whom she highly admired and respected. As it turns out, she made her most radically life-changing decision in her late thirties, and it has guided her life course ever since. Her new career turned out to be the vehicle of her survival and growth; it is no wonder that she wants to continue working through her third age. Her work has made her who she is today. She loves her work, and she loves who she is becoming as she shapes and redefines it.

The eldest of six children, Faye grew up in the Midwest, graduating from high school in a class of eighteen. Her father, a small business owner and an entrepreneur, became both a role model for her and her greatest fan. Her mother, on the other hand, was religiously strict, and an alcoholic. Originally, Faye was interested in a career as a dietician but abandoned the idea when she realized that she "couldn't hack the chemistry." She graduated from a liberal arts college with a BA in history and took a job teaching seventh and eighth grade in a small town in the Midwest. As a young woman embarking on her first career, she recalled that her father repeatedly told her, "There's nothing you can't do."

After teaching for three years, Faye was sought out by a small college to work as a recruiter. At the time most college recruiters were men, and so she was initially reluctant to leave the safety and security of her teaching position. However, the admissions director at the college urged her to give it a try, encouraging her, much as her father had done, with, "You can do anything." She joined the recruiting team of five (herself and four guys) and traveled all over the country by herself for several years. It was a challenging, rewarding experience for her.

> As I traveled from city to city, from school to school, from interview room to interview room, I rarely met *any* other women recruiters. I began to feel like I was a genuine pioneer. But with the encouragement I received from the

admissions director and my father, I never once doubted that I was going to excel at what I was doing. After a while, I'd volunteer for assignments that the four guys didn't want; I mean, I went on some hard road trips to remote locations. I guess the guys thought these trips would discourage me, but they had the opposite effect. I began to believe that what my father and the admissions director had been telling me was not so much hooey: I *could* do anything. From then on I'd do whatever the guys didn't want to do because I knew I'd get the job done. And I always did.

While working as a recruiter, Faye met her first husband, got married, and had two daughters. After eight years of marriage, Faye and her husband divorced, leaving her with two young daughters. During that time she had returned to teaching seventh and eighth grade in a small town in the Midwest. But teaching was not doing it for her, and living in the same town as her ex-husband presented challenges of a different sort. Faye was about to make a decision that changed the rest of her life. She packed up, bundled up her two girls, and moved a thousand miles away to a major metropolitan area close to where her parents were living at the time. She told us in no uncertain terms, "I was going nuts. I knew I just had to get out."

When she originally settled into her new home, she was considering returning to teaching, but a breakfast visit with the admissions director from the college where she had recruited changed that idea. The admissions director had become her mentor, and he encouraged her to try something completely new. Faye's dad had been a realtor in that metropolitan area, and so she decided to give real estate a try: "I thought to myself, why not?" Faye withdrew her teacher's pension and borrowed twenty-five hundred dollars to live on so that she could study real estate. She passed the real estate exam and hit the streets, initially working for the brokerage for which her landlord's daughter worked. Success did not come right away.

During my first year as an agent, I didn't sell a thing. Zero. But I had no doubt that I was going to be successful. To make ends meet that first year I also worked as a hostess at a restaurant—but I kept working at the real estate. I studied sales techniques and listened to sales gurus and motivational tapes. I worked my tail off: I'd work late Saturday night at the restaurant and then be up early Sunday morning to get ready to show houses. In year two, things took off, and I haven't looked back since.

Her landlord's daughter not only introduced her to her first real estate brokerage, she also introduced Faye to her current husband, Mike. During her second marriage Faye has been sustaining a delicate balance between career and family. Her family, especially her two daughters, continues to be the focal point of her life: "My girls drive me. They're mine. I made sure they had piano lessons, got to travel in Europe, and went to college." Balancing a third age career and family has led to a third age life portfolio comprised of several different vital components. In addition to the considerable time she spends working, she now allows more time for traveling and reading. She also gives more time to play and friendships. Like the others in this chapter, people have come to play an increasingly important role in Faye's life. Once a month she gets together with eleven other women to play Bunco, a round-robin dice game that serves mainly as an opportunity to catch up with neighbors, enjoy good food and drink, and giggle until silly without fear of being reproved by repressed males. Working and playing with family, friends, and neighbors make her soul sing.

As I've gotten older, I've come to identify more and more with my dad, who worked literally up until the day he died at seventy-nine. He also loved his work and refused ever to leave it. On his deathbed he told me that he was worried about a deal he was working on. He did not want his customer to be left in the lurch because he had died. I promised my dad that I would take care of his customer, and then he was at peace. How's that for customer service! Like my dad, I love what I do. It's the people. I've always worked with and around people, whether teaching, or recruiting, or selling real estate. In what I do now I get to meet new, interesting people every single day. That's a wonderful rush for me. It's just great to be meeting interesting people all the time. I'm not ready to give it up. So I'm not going to.

Faye's only regret about her professional development is that her girls had to go through those tough times with her. As she has grown older, she's put more breathing room in her life schedule, to pay more attention to what she wants and needs. Although she does not subscribe to a formal exercise regime, she sustains a vital lifestyle by walking "miles a day" showing clients prospective homes. She describes herself as a spiritual person, but she does not verbalize her spirituality. For Faye, spirituality is a private communication with God, and she prays regularly. Earlier in life she got by more often than not by "flying by the seat of my pants." Today, she finds herself spending more time reflecting and thinking ahead so that she can balance her third age career, travel with Mike, social connections with friends and neighbors, and time for herself. The result is a new sense of a successful life.

Now is the happiest time of my life. Maybe it's because when you've been through troubled times like I have, you appreciate blessings in a deeper way than if they had come more easily. I feel better now than in my forties and fifties. How are you supposed to feel at sixty? I draw a lot of energy from my work, from my travel, and from family and friends. I feel fantastic!

Faye is on the way to developing a balanced third age life portfolio. She works nearly fulltime with no plans to retire. But like the others, she has embraced a transition from a second age framework to an expanding, personally fulfilling third age lifestyle. She is pursuing third age careers not because she has to, but rather because she loves the work and treasures the opportunities it provides her to meet interesting people. The income from her third age careers enables her to play and travel in a way that enriches her identity.

FOUR LESSONS FROM THIRD AGERS STILL WORKING

ON THE SURFACE IT MAY APPEAR that these four people have outright rejected retirement or postponed it so as to keep working after all these years. Yet, each one of them has in fact been redefining her or his retirement and work to fit more closely with the person she or he is choosing to become. For them at this point in their lives, retirement is not a fixed stage but an emerging process of renewal. Not a finish line, but a new set of starting blocks.

They regard this phase of their lives as one of transition and new growth. They have been incorporating retirement ideals—more freedom, fun, and adventure—into their working lives. As Joan indicated, she has been designing her life while working to express values that are most important to her. By redesigning their work these people have been building third age careers, what Dan called his "post-career career." Third age careers have come to serve both as a form of self-expression and as a vehicle for maintaining and building personal connections. Work not as labor, but rather work as a passage to a new identity, as service, as love. This new kind of personal development is part of the promise offered to you should you choose to respond creatively to the opportunity of a fulfilling third age.

DO WORK THAT **MATTERS**

Some third agers continue to work either because they need current income or because they are strengthening personal financial stability; but the people we've followed keep on working because their work has become a major way to express who they want to become. They *are* their work in the third age, because they have chosen to do what they love. Work represents one principal form of self-expression and individual creativity. It's major way to experience flow, a space in their lives in which their soul sings. And it's part of their legacy.

Dan feels great pride at being able to help his company negotiate a major organizational transformation during a turbulent time in the marketplace. What he is doing *matters* because he is making it *matter*. For Joan work serves as a way to stimulate her growth, meet new people, and make contributions that matter. At sixty-five Carl chose to become a chaplain trainee in order that he may minister to the sick and dying, a calling toward which he has been moving during his third age. More than anything he did during his first four careers, Carl's fifth career involves work that matters. Faye's work as a real estate agent invigorates her because it continually connects her with new, interesting people and because it gives her the chance to help her clients with an endeavor that matters, finding a new home. All these people are taking advantage of opportunities provided by the third age, and are doing work that matters. That's how they define success. Determining the criteria for what matters is a personal choice and must flow from your vision for yourself after fifty.

FIND NEW WAYS TO WORK

Some people have shaped third age careers in response to what they feel to be a calling heard after their second age careers concluded. Work is a way to nurture and express a sense of self and a deepening spirituality. For all of them work is part of their creative process of life shaping. It holds a prominent place in a life portfolio that includes activities, interests, and relationships.

Dan agreed to his third age career only because he was able to build in the time he wanted to do other things. Joan has inserted flexibility into the design of her work to move her in the direction of her third age identity. Her occupations as leader, facilitator, and editor give her the chance to keep redesigning what she does every time she does it. Carl has found in his calling as a hospital chaplain an opportunity that integrates spiritual currents that have been coursing through his life for twenty years. Faye also has flexibility as an independent real estate agent and can for the most part shape her work calendar to suit her goal of meeting and enjoying new people. As recommended in chapter 3, she fits work to her life, not her life to her work.

BE GREEK: STAY BALANCED

Ah, those Greeks! Sure, they thought the sun revolved around the earth, but weren't they right about the golden mean? In shaping a third age life portfolio, the four people we met in this chapter have created a more balanced lifestyle than they did in their second age. What struck us most about Dan is how balanced he has *made* his life today. It did not happen by accident. Dan has taken and continues to take specific steps to ensure that his post-career career stays in balance. In a similar manner, Joan has worked conscientiously to design balance into her life: university work, learning and writing, connections with people, play, gardening, intellectual and spiritual growth, grandmothering, and community service. She is weaving together a rich, brightly colored, intricate self-tapestry—not a monochrome bedsheet. Although deeply involved in his studies for the chaplaincy, Carl is balancing his vocational aspiration with involvement with his family, playing the guitar, and playing and teaching bridge. He has come to recognize that perfection is not a solid black triangle at the end of a project line on a Gantt chart but rather an indirect consequence of living a balanced lifestyle.

The Jesuit theologian Pierre Teilhard de Chardin called our destiny the *omega point*, the time of utter unification, the moment of the oneness with the universe, oneness with the Creator. Our emerging self-awareness in creative balancing points us in this unifying direction, to an experience of personal integration that is the core of integrity. Faye is engaged in an on-going process of balancing the activities in her life. She has never done things by formula, but in her third age she has come to recognize that she must pay attention to how all her activities affect each other. She has enthusiastically become ringmaster of her own life.

Whatever you're comfortable with calling it—the golden mean, a balanced lifestyle, holism, or the omega point—recognize that finding a way to live *it* is crucial to your prospering in your third age.

BUILD CONNECTIONS TO PEOPLE OF ALL AGES

One of the principal reasons many third agers pursue third age careers is to maintain and expand connections with other people. They build relationships with a diversity of people, not only with people of their own age, their own gender, their own race, or their own profession. The four third agers in this chapter all *work at* mixing with people of all ages.

Dan's best friend is six years older than he is, and yet he finds stimulation in helping young leaders build the field sales force of the future for his company. Joan ensures that she surrounds herself with a variety of people, including colleagues, students, and grandchildren much younger than herself. Carl's new work as a hospital chaplain brings him into contact with people of all ages, and his desire to broaden his ministerial activities will continue to widen his circle of relationships. Faye's love of the real estate profession stems from the unceasing opportunities it gives her to meet new people of all kinds.

Birds of a feather may proverbially flock together, but the successful third agers in our study seem to underscore the advantages of disregarding that cliché, for they go out of their way to fly with as many different kinds of birds as they can. Successful third agers not only have wisdom to share, but they also have a lot to learn, from people of all ages. With a tip of the fedora to former GE leader, Jack Welch, third agers must appreciate, value, and cultivate *boundarylessness.*

Boundaryless learning. Boundaryless relationships. Boundary-less creativity.

Like Dan, clear your mind of clutter—then listen to the host of diverse voices that can and will enrich your life.

CHAPTER SEVEN

DESIGNING A THIRD AGE LIFE PORTFOLIO

Work, like you don't need the money,
Love, like you've never been hurt,
Dance, like no one is watching.

—ANONYMOUS

WHAT MAKES YOUR SOUL SING?

TO CELEBRATE HIS EIGHTIETH BIRTHDAY, President George H. W. Bush jumped with an Army parachute team from thirteen thousand feet above his presidential library. After landing he said, "This was a real thrill for me. The feeling is incredible. It's been a great day!" He made his first jump during World War II, when he was twenty. This skydive was his fifth, earning him parachutist's wings. He'd like to do another some time. Not only did he jump for excitement, he wanted to send a message that "at eighty years old, you've still got a life."

The people we've been tracking for this book have sent a similar message, that in our fifties, sixties, and seventies we have a lot more life to live than stereotypical images of aging have led us to imagine. None of our storytellers has jumped from an airplane, as far as we know, but all of them tell tales of exhilaration. Their lives radiate a youthful spirit, vibrancy, and delight in both pleasant surprises and unexpected accomplishments. As we have asked, "What makes your soul sing?" we have heard reports of joy, excitement, thrill, and passion. Behind their joy we have found encouraging lessons to help design a fulfilling third age.

There is no one right way to go about creating the life your want after fifty. As we have seen, each person has told a unique story. Over the years, however, the paradoxical six principles of growth and renewal have been operating as third age pioneers have redefined retirement, changed course, and redesigned their lives. Especially as they apply the core principle, redefining personal identity, they have been affirming an inalienable right to shape their own pursuit of happiness. Modern jargon puts it: "Follow your bliss; do what you love; have more fun in life." Not to mention that Boomer mantra, "Do your own thing." Even, "Have a great day!"

We use the latter greeting mindlessly everyday. But the words say something wonderful. Think about it. If you were to follow that expression, how would you structure your time so that you could say as you're climbing into bed, "I have had a great day"? What would you want to include? Who would be there? What would you do? Where? For how long? Do you have a few things you would want to include, or do you have a list of passionate interests like the people we've been listening to? Take time and reflect on how you can finish these two sentences:

I want to become a person who ....

To have a great day, I choose to ....

The first will express a guiding vision. The second will empower you to make that vision a reality. As you apply your answers, you will find yourself on a course of renewal.

An organization in San Francisco that helps healthcare professionals experience renewal before burnout has designed an online measurement to determine how you spend your time. Their ten questions in a *Renew-O-Meter* can help you assess where you might be coming up short as you try to plan your great days. How much time in a day do you devote to your own interests? How many times in the past week have you spent with family and friends? How many dinners have you had with them? How well have you listened? How often do you feel trapped? When did you last risk doing something new? When was the last time you encouraged or thanked someone? How many times did you laugh this week? Take their free assessment online, or make up your own. It's like taking your *soul pressure*. The questions point you towards areas in your life where your soul might sing. We have been suggesting questions and ideas throughout this book to help increase your awareness of areas that may need nurturing.

One idea we like in thinking about adding quality and putting zest into our lives is expressed in the term *flow*. In over forty years of studies of creativity and happiness, the psychologist Mihaly Csikszentmihalyi has discovered that people are happiest when completely engaged in an endeavor that challenges their talents, meets core needs, and promotes their growth. He calls this optimal experience *flow*. We also noted earlier that his studies of creative people illustrate how they tapped their creativity to sustain flow. In a recent book for business leaders, he encourages them to put more flow into their work on a daily basis. Like him we've been saying, "Put more flow into your life," and especially into whatever you think of as retirement. This redirection of energy often starts by paying more attention to your feelings and basic inclinations. What's your passion? Navigating life after fifty requires learning to know and manage yourself better. That task points to the question at the heart of shaping a new identity: "Who do you intend to become?" In asking, you are seeking not only to uncover what is within you, but also to discover the self you can create. Csikszentmihalyi states, "Knowing oneself is not so much a question of discovering what is present in oneself, but rather of creating who one wants to be." Well, it's both, isn't it?

As we have said, the people who have been showing *that they have a life* have been discovering and tapping creative resources and creating the person they want to become. As they change course and put more flow into their lives, they find more and more experiences in which their souls sing. How do you get beyond the sermon: become the person you want to be? Most of us need practical guidelines and concrete steps to take. Working on a vision of who you want to become is fundamental, especially as you work your way towards retirement.

We have suggested ways of doing that both in this and the last book. Reject stereotypes, imagine a desirable future, dream big, and affirm what you want, and what's most important to you. Next step: your vision needs to be applied to a whole life. In the past six years we've learned from our research that you can accomplish this goal by designing a third age life portfolio. Virtually all the people in this book have been doing that, often without being conscious of it. It's not their term, but our term names the process.

In this chapter we'll focus on two individuals who have been reflecting on who they want to become and who have been realizing their vision by designing unique life portfolios for nearly twenty years. The reflection that's necessary to imagine a fulfilling third age differs from the kind of thinking and planning we used to build a career in second age. Then we clarified goals, established steps and milestones, and chartered a course, the straighter the better. But managing the process of growth after fifty is more complex. The principles are paradoxical, and the intentions run in different directions simultaneously. Coursing through the Rockies in north central Colorado, an unusual river provides a helpful metaphor. Unlike the single current of most rivers or canals, the waters of this river travel in many different trajectories before joining in the final stream. The American Indians gave it the enduring name Eagle River, because its many tributaries resemble an eagle's wing. As you fashion the self you want to become in your third age, you need to decide how you want your life to flow. Like an arrow? Or like an eagle's wing?

Susan: *What I envision in retirement—or protirement—is the financial freedom to do what I want. I'm not sure I'll get there in this economy. So, I'm trying to live and do as much as I want now—so that my life already has those elements that I'm looking forward to in protirement.*

At sixty-four Susan had no specific plans to retire. Eventually, she said, she will design for herself a *protirement*, "A continuation of how I've been and lived up to now—without the financial pressure." At sixty-eight she was still working part time as a principal of her consulting group, which focuses on leadership and organizational development. In addition to paid employment, the passion she brings to work reaches in many directions. Like other third agers she has been redefining herself and her work as part of an ongoing journey of profound personal transformation. To understand that transformation, we need to go back to the beginning of a fascinating story.

Susan grew up in a large Catholic family rooted in a small midwestern town. One of seven children, she shone as a bright, energetic, ambitious student who achieved top grades and attained leadership positions—president of her class and the student council—and an award for outstanding student leader. She excelled in *over-achievement*, and aspired to become someone important, a person who would make a difference. But at that time there were not many doors open to young women. Searching in college for a meaningful career, she had a religious experience that she felt was "a call from God to do something great for the world." While growing up in a devout Catholic environment, she had been impressed with the sisters in her parish and at her college. Responding to her "deeply personal experience of mystery," she acted on what she felt was a calling by joining these women as a member of a religious community. This choice marked the beginning of "a personal and spiritual liberation."

As a nun, after graduating from college, Susan taught high school for twelve years, and then worked in campus ministry at a major state university, where she became director of learning and liturgy at the Newman Center. Sensing a need to be freer to develop her potential, she left the religious order after twenty-three years and embarked on a career in nonprofits and business. She worked for a few years in a career development organization for women in transition and a few years as director of a management institute at a community college. That position led her into the training and development division in a large financial organization, where she soon became vice president of corporate learning and organization development.

When the bank merged, she left to start another career by forming her own business. For over a dozen years she has been consulting on organization development and change, with a focus on leadership development that includes executive coaching. She views her secular work over the past twenty years as part of her own personal, spiritual development, and a primary vehicle for her own on-going learning and growth. Shortly before concluding her ten-year career as a bank vice president, Susan had a bout with ovarian cancer. Profoundly shaken as she underwent a hysterectomy, this experience emerged as another turning point in her life and eventually her career. She began to think of every day as "a second chance to live life more meaningfully and with a greater sense of purpose—to become more healed and whole both physically and in my very being." During her recovery she heard about a study tour to Greece and Crete to explore ancient goddess civilizations. Intrigued by this exploration of the feminine, she joined the tour, an experience that turned out to be a transformative pilgrimage. During the explorations of caves of the goddess she felt that she was

> journeying home to my true nature of wholeness and integrity. Walking with other women, carrying torches down the spiraling narrow paths into an enormous dark cave, I felt, in a profound way, that I was circling back down the same spiral path my female ancestors had traveled. My journey became part of theirs. I was relearning who I am, being born again through my discovery and embrace of both the power and vulnerability of the feminine within me.

Touched by the tour, she knew she had begun another segment in her spiritual journey, one that would continue her healing and unleash her feminine potential. She later realized that her cancer had been "a little death that led to a greater awareness and appreciation of all the gifts of life." In this transformative healing she was forming a new, positive view of herself and her life—giving birth to a positive third age identity. In her fifties Susan was changing course, not only in her work but also in trying to bring what she calls the divine feminine into her everyday life. She envisioned herself becoming more of a woman as she was becoming a more complete person. She began to explore other spiritual traditions that revealed a deeper feminine reality, including paganism (the goddess), American Indian beliefs and practices, Buddhism, and creation spirituality, as well as aspects of Christianity that had not been part of her previous religious education. Growing up as a good child of patriarchy, she felt that she had been forced to disown a part of herself. Now, after a dozen years on this quest for the divine feminine in herself and all creation, Susan feels that her

> movement towards the immanence of the divine feminine in all of creation, my reclaiming the goddess image and all she says to my soul, is part of my journey to discover my "original medicine." In this process I have become unlike others in my family. As I differentiate, I become better able to participate in the creation of myself—to discern my true nature and make choices to become more fully who I am.

As we have seen in other stories, learning to create the self you want to become is a key to your third age growth and renewal. Susan's enlarging sense of self has been influencing her entire life, including how she views her work and shapes her career.

During the past ten years she has been developing several third age careers, one of which is as an independent consultant, facilitator, and coach. In this career she earns income. Like tributaries of the Eagle River, however, her work spills into nonprofit activities. Susan has found or created numerous opportunities to express the feminine principles that she believes are at the core of the self she wants to become. Working in both large organizations and small non-profits, she strives to provide leadership consistent with her core values. She helps her clients work in partnerships, respectful of the whole person, with gender and diversity equity, and with sensitivity, awareness, and intention. In every aspect of her work, she believes she can incorporate feminine principles of creativity, communion, and collaboration.

As an example of how she incorporates feminine principles in paid work, she told us about a project for a company of eighteen thousand employees. Senior executives wanted to increase bench strength and improve retention of high potential managers. Susan designed and facilitated for thirty-two managers a mentoring program to encourage appreciative, collaborative relationships, humanize their work environment, and improve achievement. After a yearlong program, many of these managers said that the experience was life changing, that they became better people with their co-workers, families, friends, and communities. While learning to improve the operation of the company, they also learned to value and embrace themselves and their gifts to, and from, the world. Susan's holistic approach to this company's culture and its leadership contributed to each individual's experience of wholeness. Results like this encourage her to believe she can integrate core principles with all her third age careers. Like others we have learned from, Susan designs her work to fit the self she aspires to become.

The scope of Susan's work has broadened during the past decade, consistent with the increasing complexity of her vision. She has embraced learning, growth, and community building as key values in both her personal development and her choices of work. In addition to consulting with large organizations, she has been volunteering her services to two new small companies, helping them through initial phases. She has also formed a dialogue-learning group of women colleagues for mutual support, and she has expanded her volunteer work, with a focus on women. For example, recently she has been working with a nonprofit organization to help women increase their economic viability and with another to develop women leaders. She has also been involved with an environmental organization dedicated to restoration of water and land in the region where she lives.

A dozen years earlier, as Susan began to sense the emergence of a new self, she concluded that she needed to relocate. She believed she would be better situated in a village in a beautiful location, close to water and a forest. Following this vision, she moved out of a major metropolitan area and into a new home in a river village, where she lives within a housing cluster in which residents promote environmental consciousness. Here she serves as chair of the neighborhood association board, and her leadership helps residents engage in activities to build community and take care of the environment. This is a place she has grown to love. Though she does not now have a partner, she feels complete and free in many ways.

> I've been able to create much of what I've wanted. I live by woods and water because that became part of my vision of myself. I am contributing to the good of the world in my own ways—and that is part of my vision. I have loving friends and family, and that, too, is what I want. And I'm growing in wisdom and a sense of compassion for myself and for the world—a kind of acceptance and joyfulness in being present to what is.

In establishing a new home, she is creating the new self that integrates a key paradox in third age growth: affirming what she wants while dedicating herself to others. As her evolving life and work become more complex, Susan has been building a robust third age life portfolio. She explained how she balances her third age careers with her growth and play activities. Her list of flow activities expands into:

- Intellectual pursuits—reading books and a return to graduate school;

- Going to the movies and watching a few good shows on television;

- Physical activities—walking, biking, hiking, swimming, and canoeing;

- Entertaining friends at home;

- Participating in women's circles, sharing and celebrating stories, laughing together, and connecting with nature and with each other;

- Participating in personal development workshops;

- Playing and hanging out with nephews, nieces, and godchildren;

- Celebration, prayer, meditation, and reflection;

- Writing poetry;

- Traveling and another spiritual pilgrimage; and,

- Fun, laughter, and caring for a beautiful home.

Susan's portfolio also includes loving relationships with family, friends, and neighbors. While recovering from cancer, she felt a deep sense of support and love from her large family and expansive circle of friends, without which she believes she would not have recovered. Spending time with friends and family reinvigorates her. Entertaining them in her home is something she loves to do. Sometimes that becomes a stretch, like a recent Christmas celebration to which she sent out forty-five invitations. In addition to a large circle of intimate friends, she has grown to love grandmothering the many children in her life. She knows, she has said, that she is nothing without all the others. "I thrive because of them. I realize that love is all that matters." Part of her vision, she once said, is to love herself and others into being. Her emerging portfolio is in large part shaped by an expansion of love.

Susan is keenly devoted to caring for her own health and wellbeing. Keeping healthy has become another primary goal in her third age life portfolio, especially since recovering from cancer and a subsequent near-death experience from complications related to a ruptured appendix. For years after recovery she kept a strict vegetarian diet, eating only organic foods and shunning sugar and alcohol. In the past few years she has relaxed that, but continues to eat in a healthy way. She is committed to exercise, even though she admits she doesn't much like it. It's how she feels afterwards that motivates her. She walks several miles four or five times a week and has been doing weight training two or three times a week for over ten years. For the past year she has been actively involved in an exercise regimen that has strengthened and greatly improved her bone density. Susan goes to Yoga once a week, does postures at home, and attends workshops focused on movement and dance as well. In part, her pledge to self-care aims to sustain her wellbeing, but it is also intended to retain strength and agility as she ages.

I resent the negative stereotypes of aging in our culture.
It's all a bunch of hooey. I don't think of myself as old or
feeble or diminished. There's lots I want to do, explore,
and give before I die. I hope I have time to do it all. I feel
some aches and pains and know I have to work with them
and take care of them lovingly. I get up each day with a
strong sense of gratitude and hope. I work on staying
strong and healthy, because I want to be able to move the
watering hose and carry my groceries into my nineties.

Susan feels she has a third of her life in front of her, and
she's set ninety-six as an age to reach. After her third age, she
hopes to experience vital aging in her fourth age.

Many of Susan's activities fall outside the boundaries of
what you may have been taught to expect of a woman near
seventy. Not the least of these endeavors is her ongoing dedication to learning, another significant part of her life portfolio. Besides keeping up in her field and reading novels, Susan
entered a doctoral program in creation spirituality, where
several times a year she has traveled to attend courses. In
between the sessions she has read books and articles and
written lengthy papers. She is now completing this program
in time to receive her doctorate when she's seventy. In this
full schedule she also makes time for her hobby, writing poetry. Always intellectually keen, age has not dulled the knife; it
seems to have made it sharper.

Susan sees her life as a spiral, going round and round at
deeper levels of awareness and affirmation. As her life circles
around a core of commitments and possibilities and expands
in new directions, she experiences continued transformation.
Because she abhors the cultural degradation of older people,
and in particular the degradation of older women, she wants
to affirm her own worth and the value of older women everywhere as she pursues her vision, continues her work, and

sustains her growth. While she has earned more money and achieved more public recognition than some other members of her family, she does not see economic achievement, nor her leadership positions and accomplishments in work, nor her beautiful home and lifestyle, as the most important signs of her success. Like others in our study, Susan has been redefining success.

> I can point to several measures of apparent success. But the measure of real success, the only thing that counts in the long run, is that I have gained the love and affection of my family and friends, that I have loved and contributed something of good to them and to this world. And that I have lived up to my full potential—that I have grown in consciousness and compassion to the fullest extent of my capability. I have miles to go on that path before I sleep. That's why I need and want so many more years.

As we were working on this chapter, Susan sent us a paper that expresses her ongoing vision of her evolving self. It is a fitting way to conclude her remarkable story.

> Paradoxically, as I grow older and become more able to make my own growth-filled choices, I also become more able to realize my place in the interdependent web of life. I know that I am nothing without everything else. I have a responsibility to move outward and to extend myself into the world in service of justice and compassion. The archetypal feminine is ultimately life giving. I hope I have many years left on this planet to deepen my heart's knowing of this amazing gift of life and love, and to live in service to restoring it to the world.

This vision of herself as she grows older reflects a deep sense of integration and purpose; it suggests a spiraling process that has reconnected with a young woman's vision of "doing something great for the world." As Susan envisions her future for the next twenty-five years, her evolving third age life portfolio will keep her moving ahead to become the person she aspires to be, to redefine retirement, and to leave a legacy that enriches both those she loves and the world.

Ted: *I have a wonderful life. Being semiretired feels like a promotion— giving me time to focus on what I love. This is about as ideal an arrangement as I can imagine.*

Ted's story was in chapter 8 in *The Third Age*. At the time of the last interview before publication he was sixty-two, a busy professional with a full life. As with most stories in that book, the pattern of his life unfolded like a living mosaic, with shifting contours, varying shades of light and dark, and changing elements within a recognizable frame. From nearly any vantage point, his life could have been deemed successful, but that result was in large part because he had redefined success based on factors not often found in a resume. If anything, you could consider his life now even more successful, using the metrics of personal growth, health, happiness, creative balance, contribution, accomplishment, and love. To get to this enviable situation, Ted had earlier learned that he had to renew and reshape his life course.

When Ted finished his graduate degree in architecture in his midtwenties, he joined a Boston firm that he has been with for over forty years. His specialty, landscape architecture, has played an important role in the enlargement of the firm. During his first twenty years there he was over-committed to career success, putting in hundred-hour weeks, traveling much of the time, and seeing little of his first wife and three young children. After twelve years in his first marriage, he became divorced; he then met and subsequently wed Ellen. They never had children of their own, but they included Ted's three children in their lives. And Ted's son lived with them during high school. But early in his second marriage, his life was still focused on achievement at work. At forty-eight he experienced a turning point that has changed the course of his life.

Ted was invited to go on an eight-day Outward Bound course, which proved to be both exhilarating and eye opening. During the final solo period, his reflection led him to realize that his "life was out of whack." He sketched out a four-point program to renew his life and bring it into balance. He later referred to his life plan as a four-legged stool. At this point the stool was about to topple over, because all the weight was on one leg, his career. In that moment he made a commitment to put emphasis on the other three legs: his family and marriage, community service, and self-care and play. In an interview five years later, at age fifty-four all four legs had been installed in a balanced, renewed life.

Ted's work continued to be exciting and fulfilling. A tour of his office with large photos showing the imaginative design and beauty of many projects gave testimony to his continuing creative output. But in his work he was learning to take different risks than he had during the first twenty-five years: "I might tell a client that I can't fit his request into my schedule—or that I can't make a meeting because of a family reunion." He would never have taken that position earlier. His enlarged set of priorities was shaping the way he spent his time.

His second marriage, which he said had begun to go sour during his forties, took on new life. On different occasions from his midfifties through his sixties he has said, "We have an incredibly close marriage—a wonderful relationship."

When asked at sixty-two what scared him most he responded without hesitation, "The thought of losing my wife." Several years after his Outward Bound course, they decided to realize a dream of building their own home on a Maine island. They found the island and started camping on it to learn its seasons. The beautiful home they built represents a metaphor of their marriage—a joint venture, with lots of sharing, open space, innovation, compromises, and comfort. For the first ten years they used it as a weekend and summer retreat; they have since moved in to make it a home. In the past fifteen years their marriage has flourished. They recently reported celebrating their thirty-third anniversary by doing autumn outdoor sketching and painting together on the lovely, rugged Maine island of Monhegan.

While balancing work and family, Ted was also developing the leg of community service. For years he has been serving as an Outward Bound trustee, as well as a member on a number of boards related to environmental enhancement and conservation. Through his fifties and early sixties he was giving himself as generously as time allowed to public-interest projects. And he was giving more attention to taking care of himself and finding time to play. As a former athlete, he has always enjoyed sports. He designed a healthy lifestyle and regularly worked out, swam, played tennis and golf, skied, and sailed.

Ted's life design was part of a process of redefining his identity. In his early fifties he was proud of being a partner, with his name on the firm's letterhead. But as the number of partners increased, the firm decided to remove all names except those of the founders. At first that hurt. But Ted began to realize that his measure of success was no longer to be found in external signs and status symbols but rather in the quality of experience, personal growth, contributions, and relationships. A sense of third age leadership was emerging as he focused on the areas most important to him. He was redefining work, putting more emphasis on creativity, his contributions to urban renewal and environmental enhancement, and mentoring. In the final interview before the last book, he drew a design of his life.

His long-term purpose is to bring together the significant aspects of his life into balance. He sketched a river with four major and several minor tributaries. Work remained an important source of flow; marriage, family, friendships, community service, self-care, and play were others. In retrospect, it appears that he had designed the flow of his life to be like an eagle's wing. At sixty-two Ted's development illustrated the creative alternative to conventional aging by initiating second growth in the third age.

In conversations at that time Ted had no plans to retire— he didn't like the word and couldn't see it applying to him. As he passed sixty-five he began to have second thoughts. His colleagues in the firm were beginning to retire. One day they're in; the next day they're out. It was all or nothing. Ted was attracted by the idea of having more freedom, especially the chance to have more time with Ellen at their Maine home. But he loved his work too much to give it up completely. So he explored an option no one else had. He negotiated a semiretirement package that enabled him to reduce his days in the office and focus on the aspects of his work he loved most, the ones to which he felt he could make the greatest contribution.

After five years he was still the only one to have made such an arrangement. The firm has no policy on semiretirement, but the deal has given him the opportunity and support he needs to succeed in his experiment. It is a win-win agreement. He keeps contributing to both on-going and new projects, with time to give of himself in other ways outside the firm. He says he has to be careful not to overstep his boundaries or stay away too long, since he now reports to his son, who has risen to a responsible position in the firm. Ted is not merely working half time. He has truly redefined his work, developing several third age careers that serve the firm, his profession, other institutions, his community, and society as a whole. At sixty-seven he said,

About two years ago I became semiretired. I'm still trying to get used to it. Actually, I feel better about it now. I love my work and hate the idea of retirement if it means I would be without it. I'm going in Tuesday, Wednesday, and Thursday usually. But I'm still flying to projects. I'm going to Denver this week; last week it was Ohio, where I've been involved in a big project on Cincinnati's waterfront. I did stuff like this before, but now I'm more focused. I'm deeply involved in urban renewal and design with a strong commitment to improving the environment.

Other projects have taken him to upstate New York and to Los Angeles. At last report he was excited about a different kind of project, one that would take him and his wife to China: "Our next big project is to work on the 2008 Olympics in Beijing. Ellen will go along for some of it. She speaks a little Chinese. We're not sure how involved we'll be, but we're sure looking forward to it. It's a huge task to get ready for something on this scale—and exciting."

It doesn't take much imagination to understand why Ted didn't want to leave his work behind in retirement. In listening to him describe his favorite projects, you could hear his soul singing. Work still is one of the core aspects of who he is and who he yet wants to become. It has only become more satisfying since he's designed this third age career:

I've always enjoyed my work. Being semiretired means I'm
out of the politics, which I don't like. Actually, this seems
like a promotion. I have time to focus on what I love. This is
about as ideal an arrangement as I can imagine. My son has
joined the firm and become a partner. I've enjoyed bringing
him along. Much of my time in the firm recently has been
spent mentoring young architects, and teaching them.

While this arrangement has been soul satisfying to Ted, it
has also contributed to the ongoing success of the firm. The
organization benefits from his creativity, expertise, and experience in developing new projects. And it now has a built-in
support system for its young professionals, who stand to gain
enormously from the mentoring Ted provides. As you read in
chapter 6, a new kind of contractual arrangement for third age
leaders and professionals will benefit not only individuals,
but also organizations and society. What are needed are the
skills of third age planning, with a focus on third age careers.

The teaching Ted has practiced informally in the firm has
spread out into educational institutions. He teaches a variety
of courses, often short-term modules or mini-courses to
graduate students and prospective architects.

Teaching is becoming more important to me. I love this,
too. I'm taking on more teaching in universities. Last
summer at Harvard I did a summer short course for people in mid-careers who are thinking about landscape
architecture. Soon I'll do a three-day workshop at the
University of Colorado with students who want to focus
on landscape architecture. I love doing this and don't
want to let it go. This kind of activity is also good for the
firm; it recruits talented, interested people they might not
otherwise have discovered. This teaching also spills into
another leg of my stool, community service.

As he redefined his career as architect, Ted has added the dimension of teacher. In both capacities, he receives income, though teaching is more of a service than an important source of revenue. But the work that spills into the community service is for free. With more free time, he can give more of himself to causes that need him.

Ted has become excited about contributing to urban renewal, especially through environmental design. When asked once about a sense of purpose, he remarked that he didn't think of himself as having a single purpose; but he takes great pride and satisfaction when visiting a site, seeing how it has been improved and provides joy to those who are using it. As he has grown, he has been developing a more caring life. Recently he has become involved in several boards that have a similar focus, some on a national scale, some local.

I'm now a trustee of the Riley Institute in Charleston. This institute is devoted to helping mayors in the United States become better urban designers. We're trying to improve our cities. It's encouraging to see mayors learn and get involved. I'm also involved in local institutions focusing on the waterfront. We're trying to protect the natural environment from development. I'm working with a Maine restoration project that is developing a garden in a space previously used by industry. In Boston I've been working on a Mystic River project. Semiretirement allows me more time, which I didn't have before, to give myself to environmental projects that I believe are important.

In addition to environmentally directed work, Ted has also become involved with professional associates on a national level. One is project at Rice University in Houston; the other is a government agency. In this work he is collaborating with his peers to establish the highest standards in architecture. He enjoys this work with professional colleagues. As Ted has clarified his core values—what he loves and cares most about—he's been able to give a sharp, consistent focus to the many forms of work that fill several third age careers: architect, professional leader, mentor, teacher, concerned citizen, and champion of urban renewal and environmental improvement. The many tributaries of his redefined work—his eagle's wing—fill a sizeable chunk of his third age life portfolio.

As he was developing a semiretired life, Ted and Ellen decided to move permanently into their Maine dream house, an hour's drive from Boston. He can put in three days midweek at the firm, spending four days with her at home. They have designed their home to support the kind of life they've long wanted. It has a large, modern kitchen suited to prepare both small meals and large ones when three adult children and spouses along with eight grandchildren arrive for long weekends and summer vacations. Ted's sister and brother-in-law and a large circle of friends, who all live close by, often help fill the expansive downstairs rooms framed by several glass walls overlooking the woods and water.

> Ellen and I moved to our Maine home a couple years
> ago—a good move. We love it here. Though the island has
> a causeway, it feels remote. We see more of our family
> here, especially in the summer. We have eight grandchil-
> dren, and we're more involved in their lives than ever.
> Many are in college around the country. The role of grand-
> parent is becoming more important; it's much bigger than
> I imagined. We're visiting grandchildren in college. When I
> fly to Colorado next week, I'll see one of them there. Their
> parents live close by, as do many friends. We see a lot of
> family and friends here. The family leg in my four-legged
> stool has grown considerably in the past few years. Being

semiretired gives me more time to be together with those I love. And to entertain friends. Come visit us—we'll take you sailing on our twenty-six-foot yawl.

This carefully designed house, with ample space for crowds, has become home or a second home to a growing number of people. It has small rooms tucked away upstairs where Ellen and Ted can have privacy to concentrate on reading, activity planning, and hobbies. Ted confessed that he's been enviously eyeing a small apartment they rent out in the back of this house, because it has a quiet room with a view, ideal to practice his hobby of drawing and painting. He and Ellen are happy spending time alone together here, enjoying the ambience and the views, and still working on this house-in-progress.

They also spend more time enjoying outdoor activities in this state that calls itself *vacationland*. Being on the coast, they're on or near the water much of the time in warm weather. Their sailboat gets regular use in summer and early fall; they also have a large, open outdoor motorboat to go exploring on nearby rivers. When the temperature drops and the snow piles up, they race out into the woods for another adventure. For several years they have been raising sled dogs, which they have trained to pull them for hours at a fast clip through the snowy forest. Once, while Ted was traveling, Ellen came to the phone sounding exhilarated, having just come from four hours of sledding with her dogs. This pursuit has become more her sport than his, but like so many other activities, they love doing it together. They also enjoy downhill skiing in the Maine mountains. And when the snow melts, and the black flies have deserted the drying forests, the two of them enjoy hiking along country lanes or through the woods. They have found, chosen, and staked out a space that makes their souls sing.

The fourth leg in Ted's stool consists of time devoted to taking care of himself and play. In his forties Ted had little time for exercise, and he had begun to drink more alcohol and eat more food than was good for him. As part of his four-point plan, he cut way down on alcohol, began to follow a healthy diet, and started a regimen of activities: swimming, tennis, workouts, golf, skiing, and hiking. Throughout his fifties he sustained a vital lifestyle. In his early sixties he developed a hip problem that therapy couldn't cure. His decision to have surgery has meant that he's had to forgo certain pastimes, but he has been able to maintain many others.

> I had a hip replaced three years ago. That triggered an awareness of how important it is to take good care of myself. It actually started a revolution in how I do it. My doctor told me I'd be better off if I was lighter. So I went on a diet and lost thirty pounds. I'm now down to where my weight should be. I'm six feet two inches and a hundred and ninety pounds—I'm in better shape than I was five or ten years ago. There are a few things that I can't do—like horseback ride, single's tennis, and black diamond ski runs. But my body is in good shape. I walk a couple of miles a day and work out in a fitness center three times a week with a bike and weights. I still love to ski: Ellen and I ski together on blue runs. We love to run with our sled dogs. I still play golf and am doing pretty well on the course. We sail and often play double's tennis. I'm getting more into fly-fishing. I now have more time to be active. I'm sixty-eight, but don't feel it. I feel a lot younger than my parents did at this age. I think they just expected to get old—and did. I love what I'm doing, my family, and my life in Maine. I have a wonderful life.

A paradox in second growth is expanding one's capacity to care, learning to balance caring for oneself with a deeper caring for others. Ted is one of the few people in this study who has consciously been designing his life to achieve a sense of balance. He first proposed to himself a four-point plan, later described his life as a four-legged stool, and once sketched his interests as a river with several tributaries. What his models amount to is what we've been calling a third age life portfolio. Ted's portfolio has been emerging, enlarging, and changing shape for nearly twenty years.

Designing such a complex life is an ongoing process. At seventy his portfolio is still packed with the six principles of growth and renewal. Ted has committed himself to work while also dedicating himself to more play and a healthy lifestyle. Time for himself is balanced with time with Ellen, his family, friends, and numerous nonprofit organizations. He has shaped a new identity, recognizing limitations of becoming older while affirming his youthful spirit. The blossoming mosaic of his portfolio life keeps getting richer and more fascinating.

FOUR LESSONS FROM PORTFOLIO BUILDERS

Let Your Flow Be Like an Eagle's Wing

A common strategy when building an artistic or financial portfolio is to diversify. When building a third age life portfolio, the same strategy applies. Diversify the flow in your life. This creative process enables you to give structure to the complexities of the person you are becoming. The self you want to become is not an entity—not a biomechanical thing in motion, but a historical process in which you become your own story. His-story, her-story, that's what each of us is shaping. As you become involved in this process, we think you'll find that you have an entirely different outlook on life after fifty and retirement.

Matthew, the professor specializing in gerontology in chapter 3 of the The Third Age, was looking forward to retirement during his sixties. He kept putting it off. As he reached sixty-five his university offered him full salary, with fewer assignments as a way of tapering down towards retirement. So he shifted gears, leaving behind administrative duties and teaching, to focus on research. By the time he was sixty-eight he could retire, which he formally did. But he found that he was still involved with colleagues in research nearly every day. They have been invited to present their findings around the world, and so he has been traveling more.

A group of seniors learned of his research and asked him to lead them in conversations about spirituality in aging, giving him a chance to apply his learning in his community. A doctoral program he helped launch asked him to teach in the methods course. Then he was invited to play a lead role in developing an international conference on aging. It's no surprise that he hasn't found time to retire. At seventy-three his emerging self is still flowing in many directions: work redefined and enlarged beyond his professional role, involvement in an expanding family (he has three granddaughters who make his soul sing), hobbies, helping his wife develop her work in a nearby city, regular exercise and sports, and time with friends and in the community. All these endeavors contribute to a diversified third age life portfolio that has redefined what Matthew once thought would be retirement.

Sometimes a rich portfolio life happens as serendipity. But Ted and Susan both have shown that it can occur by design. That's a major lesson we've learned from them. Susan said about retirement, "I'm not sure I'll get there. So I'm try-ing to live and do as much as I want now—so that my life already has those elements that I'm looking forward to." And what she wants now amounts to an impressive, highly diver-sified list of intentions and activities—work, play, love and laughter with family and friends, grandmothering, neighbor-ing, community building, learning, spirituality, exercise, time in nature, poetry writing, and travel. Her life flows in many streams, within a framework of becoming a whole person embodying, as she put it, "the archetypal feminine that is ultimately life giving."

Ted has been applying his talents as a designer to the shape of his life, directing his energies towards the things he loves and cares most about. His and Susan's portfolio lives are not set. They keep changing as new opportunities arise, and as they take risks to try new things: Ted with teaching and an activity regimen because of a hip replacement, and Susan with a doctoral program and ventures with emerging organi-zations. These and the others we've followed have surprised themselves by having so many interests after fifty. Your chal-lenge is to organize your interests into a diversified portfolio aimed at yielding your story.

FREE YOURSELF FOR WHAT'S IMPORTANT

While most people we've talked with don't like the idea of retirement, or at least the term, one aspect of the third age has wide appeal: an increase in personal freedom. The dan-ger is that we could see it primarily as freedom from the many things we're tired of doing or that have gotten in the way of important interests. As Ed learned from a retirement seminar, he needed to think about retiring *to* rather than retiring *from*. He relishes the freedom he now has to engage in a new career of raising bees and selling honey, traveling with his wife, and spending more time with friends and family. Susan is not sure she'll ever retire, but already she knows it must be a "protirement" in which she can fully express her core values. Ted finds that he has "a wonderful life" because he's much freer to do what he loves, be with those he loves, and spend time in the space he loves. "I have more time now," he tells us, to be and do things that make his soul sing and contribute to the wellbeing of individuals, cities, local communities, and nature.

One challenge you'll face in redefining retirement is to frame in a meaningful way the increase in freedom you'll experience as earlier necessities diminish. As the last tuition bills have been paid, mortgage payments decrease or cease, interest in collecting status symbols declines, and investments stop dropping over the cliff, many of us don't feel the need to increase our income. Most of us experience more freedom from career and financial pressure now that we're older. What do you want to do with this freedom?

Woody realized, when offered a much lower salary from Outward Bound, that since his daughters had graduated and the house was paid for, he and his wife didn't need as much money as they had. He understood that he was free to accept the work he loved, and he's been loving it for the past fifteen years. When his position was later eliminated, he realized again that he was free to give of himself in the equivalent of a half-time position. He has structured his freedom with flexibility that permits him to do other things he loves to do— spend time with his wife, daughters, and grandkids, travel, keep healthy, be with friends, and enjoy the cultural life of New York. Woody was "scared to death" of retirement, because it seemed like a deprivation. Since he has redefined it along the lines of transition in semiretirement, he finds the freedom exhilarating. It opens him to experiences that enable him to "make an interesting life."

Americans, ironically enough, have trouble with a lot of freedom. This country is the land of the free, where individuals celebrate an inalienable right to life and liberty, especially on the Fourth of July. But given a huge dose of freedom, most don't know what to do with it. America has more millionaires than any country, but unlike the rich elsewhere, most of our millionaires spend their lives working hard in demanding schedules. They apparently want to be like the rest of us. Leisure is not a term we are comfortable with, no matter what income bracket we're in. If you think of leisure, what do you envisage? The Greeks in classical Athens invented a notion of leisure as an opportunity for developing a full life. What gave a person leisure was not idleness but freedom with a reduction of necessity. Leisure, they believed, allows a person to escape from the constraints of *have-to* and enter the opportunity of *free-to*. That idea inspired Jefferson's famous phrase, "the pursuit of happiness." Millions of contemporary descendants have lost the true sense of leisure.

But not all contemporaries have. Look at the people in this study. They have captured a sense of expanding freedom in the process of becoming more complete persons. They are free to work—for pay or for nothing—free to contribute themselves to people and causes that matter, free to lead the way to better tomorrows, free to risk something new, and free to put more flow into their lives. Only when we're free do our souls sing.

CREATE THE RIGHT SPACE

If you think of the shaping of your life story as a drama, you'll know that your drama has to be staged on the right kind of set. Many people in this study realized that to become the persons they want to be, they had to change location.

Susan felt she needed to be in a small community, in a wooded river village; here she feels rooted, closer to nature, where she senses more readily the creative process of life. Ted and his wife dreamed of leading a fulfilling life on the coast of Maine. After years of searching, then more years of building, they have made a home that nourishes the best in both of them. After retiring as a financial officer, El (chapter 4) and his wife also moved to Maine, settling on a farm that allowed her to open an antique store and permitted him to carve and spend more time outdoors. After ten years they concluded this career and rebuilt an old hunting lodge, because they wanted to preserve in symbolic form for generations to come a set of values and way of life they had come to believe was too important to lose. As he graduated from a large corporation, Vic and his wife (chapter 4) searched across America to find and settle in a California community that provides them the opportunities they wanted to shape their commencement.

These people have not moved merely to change location or reduce mortgage payments. Their choice of space fits the self they are trying to become. "My purpose is to become the person I can be," El told us repeatedly. His relocations were designed to support that purpose, shared by his wife—and to provide both of them more opportunities to keep growing, have fun, and build a legacy. In this space El has experienced the freedom he needs to move towards his purpose. "I am still awed by the realization when I wake up that the day is mine to structure—so different from my life in the corporation," he told us several times over the last fifteen years. Half the people in this study have moved to new locations, to design the set on which their personal dramas continue to unfold.

But half have stayed in place. Yet they have also been doing set design, or redesign. Betty and her husband (chapter 4) have been working on their cottage style home for over thirty years, developing a beautiful garden into which they bring friends to celebrate and enjoy the fragrant springs of northern California. Rebecca and her husband (chapter 5) have been working on their home for forty years, making it a welcoming space of beauty, filled with her artwork. Eva (chapter 5), in redesigning her life, has also been redecorating her house and has spent many hours cultivating a garden that delights the eyes of all who pass by. The lesson all these people teach is not that it's necessary to move, but that it's important to invest yourself in designing your personal space to fit the portfolio life you are creating.

LIVE VITALLY

Our culture has flooded us with stereotypical images of life over fifty as decline and degeneration—slowing down, cutting back, and becoming a spectator of life. Susan, Ted, and the others are fighting the stereotypes.

Susan told us, "I resent the negative stereotypes of aging in our culture. It's all a bunch of hooey. I don't think of myself as old or feeble or diminished." She is an active player in life, not a spectator. For the past fifteen years she has been committed to healing, wholeness, and optimal health. She walks and hikes almost daily, does Yoga, goes to a fitness center, and attends dance workshops: "I work on staying strong and healthy, because I want to be able to move the watering hose and carry my groceries into my nineties." Daphne (chapter 8 of *The Third Age*) has maintained a similar practice for over thirty years. At seventy-six she was featured in a documentary showing her in a fitness program and a dance class, entertaining friends, and hiking through Idaho forests with a group of campers. At eighty-four she has just finished an autobiographical book about her life's work, *vital aging*. As one editor said of the book, she models what she preaches. Daphne, Susan, and the other women are showing a totally different image of becoming older—engaged, vital, healthy, and enthusiastic. They have been creating a portfolio life with impressive élan.

Ted has also rejected the stereotypes of aging as belonging to a previous generation. He feels younger at sixty-eight than he did earlier, younger by far than his parents when they were this age: "I think my parents just expected to get old and did. I'm active and loving what I'm doing." Even getting a hip replacement didn't make him sedentary. On the contrary, he followed his doctor's instructions and lost weight so that he could remain involved in outdoor activities. He cut out a few pursuits like horseback riding and expert ski trails, but he continues to hike, sail, run sled dogs with his wife, ski intermediate trails, play golf, and work out in a fitness center. Ted and others have learned to compensate for a minor disability; they have not given up but taken on new challenges.

Other men have used the freedom in a redefined retirement to achieve optimal health. Vic makes use of trails near his new home to ride a bike. Ed has more time to play sports with his sons and friends. El hikes daily with his wife, hunts and fishes with friends, and promotes a healthy lifestyle as part of his legacy. Woody now has more time to improve his health by going to a fitness center and enjoying scuba diving with his oldest grandson. At sixty-five Carl increased his daily activities, walking and going to a fitness center three times a week.

As they invest in building a diverse third age life portfolio to shape their personal stories, these men and women have made sure that they keep their spirits soaring by keeping their bodies strong and vital.

CHAPTER EIGHT

FOR THIRD AGERS
APPROACHING RETIREMENT

Scarcely anything material or established which I was brought up to believe was permanent and vital, has lasted. Everything I was sure or taught to be sure was impossible, has happened.

—CHURCHILL, *My Early Life*

CASEY NO LONGER AT THE BAT

FORTY PLUS YEARS AGO, Charles Dillon "Casey" Stengel, the torture-tongued baseball manager who in twelve years with the New York Yankees won ten pennants and seven World Series, finally—after fifty-five years in baseball—retired at seventy-five (and only because a broken hip forced him to). A couple of months after Casey had hung up his spikes, a posse of New York sportswriters bumped into Edna Stengel having lunch by herself in a diner in midtown Manhattan. The "Old Perfesser" had taken himself out of the ballpark limelight, and the sportswriters were missing the nonstop flow of

Casey-speak—"Stengelese" that had included such brain-teasers as, "I've always heard it couldn't be done, but sometimes it don't always work"; such insights as, "Good pitching will always stop good hitting and vice versa"; and such mind-benders as, "Without losers, where would the winners be?"

When fired by the Yankees after the 1960 season—good grief, the team had gone two whole seasons without winning a world championship—Casey had declared, "I'll never make the mistake of turning seventy again." Casey had always dished out great copy for Gotham's newspapers. What had the Hall-of-Famer been up to since retiring? At Edna's invitation the sportswriters pulled up chairs around her. "What's it like," they eagerly wanted to know, "having Casey home everyday?" As they tell the story, Edna took a sip of lemonade, gazed out at them, and declared, "You know, boys, I married Casey in 1924. I married him for richer and for poorer, in sickness and in health, and till death do us part." She paused and took another sip of lemonade: "But I sure in the hell didn't marry the sumbitch to have lunch with him everyday!"

We have all heard stories of fumbled, bungled, or failed retirements, disheartening accounts by family members, friends, and acquaintances. The data are striking: as many as 70 percent of retirees go back to work, either fulltime or part time, within eighteen months of having walked away from the job. 1) How come? 2) And, what are they doing? The short answers: 1) they need to, and 2) mostly the same old thing. They need the money, or they need the human connections, or they need to be doing something to keep from being bored. As you would expect, when we relate these chilling numbers to people, almost to a person each boasts, "That won't happen to me." But cocky confidence doesn't do it, and statistically roughly three out of the four of them will be proven wrong. Many people do stumble as they move into the third age. Why? And more important, will you?

FIVE BIG RISKS FOR THIRD AGERS APPROACHING RETIREMENT

MOST PEOPLE AREN'T PREPARED for leaving second age and entering third age. Many think they're ready to change course because they've been running retirement-plan numbers backwards and forwards for the better part of a half-decade or more, or because they've been scouting out prospective retirement communities by way of Internet webcams, or because they've participated in a pre-retirement workshop, or because they've watched PBS specials on diet or exercise or meditation, or because they've sat on the beach or in the mountains or on a front porch swing and stared off into space, imagining all the fun things they'll soon be doing. The *Life of Riley*.

Although people who stumble as they move into third age typically do so for a combination of reasons, our interviews suggest that five risks in particular present a gauntlet of challenges to third agers thinking about retiring:

1. *Being Clueless*: Misconceptions can trigger feelings of disorientation, displacement, and defeatism among third agers. Being clueless does have consequences.

2. *Aging Stereotypes*: Negative stereotypes of aging predispose a person to a "woe is me" mindset, subjecting third agers to a destructive self-fulfilling prophecy.

3 *Hanging On*: A "heck no, I won't go" outlook deludes a person into trying to perpetuate the achievement values of the second age into the third age.

4. *To–Do-ism*: A "to do, or not to do" obsession compels a person to activity excess, a compulsion to do. Remember, "Do be a do bee, and don't be a don't bee." Forget it.

5. *Second Age Addictions:* We are all creatures of habit. A same old, same old attitude to third age can trigger relapses into counterproductive second age behaviors.

Risk 1—Being Clueless

Most fundamental, making a successful transition from second age to third age requires people to have a down-to-earth understanding of the landscape they will encounter as they travel into their fifties, sixties, and seventies. Unrealistic expectations for navigating life after fifty can lead to disappointment and frustration, at times resentment. Feelings of disorientation, displacement, and defeatism can follow. Why? Many people simply do not take the time to get the information they need to form a levelheaded view of what it's like out there.

At a pre-retirement workshop of a major corporation, a member of a panel of recent retirees—invited back to describe what retirement was "really like"—told the following story:

> One day after having played an early round of golf, I had a brilliant idea. Wouldn't my wife just love it if I reorganized the kitchen? For thirty years I had never been able to find a darn thing in that kitchen. Well, my wife had gone off to play bridge, and so I set to work: moving pots and pans, shuffling plates and glasses, and—this was a stroke of genius—alphabetizing the pantry. When she returned, I proudly showed her what I had *done for her.* She smiled and said, "Thank you, dear." The next morning, when I got back after a round of golf, she invited me into the garage. "Look what I've *done for you,*" she announced, taking me back to my tool bench. "I've sorted all your tools—*by color.*

Here are tools with red handles, and here's the blues, and the blacks, and the silver ones are in that great big pile by the lawn mower." Then she turned and walked away. I never went in her kitchen again.

The underlying driver of being clueless is lack of information: lack of information about one's own financial status and preparedness, lack of information about where to live, lack of information about how to connect with new people, lack of information about what will fire one's spirit after fifty, lack of information about the interests and drives of one's spouse or partner, or other loved ones, and even lack of information— and we're not trying to be flip here—about information: where to go, with whom one should talk, and what questions to ask.

RISK 2—AGING STEREOTYPES

We Americans find ourselves saturated with derogatory images of aging. The prejudicial labels have fused with one another in a chain reaction to form even more belittling stereotypes. Stereotypes procreating stereotypes. We read them in newspapers, we hear them in music, and we see them in movies and on television. Consider how the grandparent characters are depicted on most television situation comedies: as over-the-hill busybodies getting in the way, commenting on their digestive-tract tribulations, and otherwise mucking things up for their children and grandchildren. Funny, and not so funny.

People who allow themselves to fall prey to these denigrating aging stereotypes are at risk of failing retirement because the disparaging images repulse them from embracing life after fifty. Sometimes these stereotypical expectations come from unexpected directions. At a third age planning workshop, a participant told the story of how one of his thirty-something daughters, a physician, had become increasingly frustrated by his third age creativity. One day she blurted out, "Dad, why don't you just act your age?" His response, "I don't wanna."

Stereotypes trigger apprehension about change, a five-alarm panic at becoming one of those over-the-hill old folks as depicted by youth-obsessed ad execs and media moguls: the "Where's the beef" granny, or the "I've fallen and I can't get up" lady, or the wrinkly gents gathered around Ray's dad in the lodge sauna in the sitcom *Everybody Loves Raymond*. Most of us are so imbued with these derisive misconceptions about aging that freeing ourselves of them takes a determined effort, because each of us has been shaped by a different mix of images and experiences with aging.

RISK 3—HANGING ON

Remember the first time you read about the Spanish explorer Ponce de Leon? Remember how pointless the Fountain of Youth seemed to you, how silly? Yet, didn't you wonder for a moment, "Wouldn't that be neat if it did exist?" And there was Frank Capra's 1937 film *Lost Horizon*, especially the scene in which the young Himalayan woman steps across the frontier of the Valley of the Blue Moon, Shangri-La, and withers in fast-forward fashion into an ashen mummy right before our movie-going eyes. In *The Lord of the Rings* the Elves are able to live forever only if they are willing to leave Middle Earth and cross over to the blessed realm of Valinor.

As illusory, and delusional, as are the Fountain of Youth, Shangri-La, and Valinor, one of the most common reasons people fail retirement is that they refuse to let go of second age. As if an environment-friendly time machine were at their disposal, they appear always to be probing for warps and creases in the space-time continuum to avoid third age. It's time to toss your "Heck no, I won't go" protest sign into the trash.

The principal driver of hanging on is most likely a concern about rejection, a fear of aging, and a deep dread of being cast out and left behind. Not that a treadmill or a vitamin cocktail or a nip and a tuck are necessarily the work of the Dark Side of the Force—who wants crows feet, telltale wrinkles, and a droopy chin? But nonstop efforts to combat the cumulative ravages of gravity, ultraviolet radiation, and greasy food and forestall the natural course are doomed to failure. The chemicals, the creams, and the potions—whether physical or psychological—form a kind of seductive aging alchemy. It's not nice to fool Mother Nature. A single-minded focus on preserving the glories of second age can prevent a person from doing the planning needed to embrace third age.

Risk 4—To–Do-ism

If the authors were to pick one symbol for the second age, it would be the *to-do list*. My goodness, there's so much to do once we get out of school, find a job, and perhaps raise a family. Endless, thankless cycles of cooking, cleaning, and straightening up; staying awake during boring meetings, writing reports, and taking customers to lunch; dealing with the cable company, making sure the lawn mower blade is sharpened, and trouble shooting a leaking station in the sprinkler system. Oh yeah, and taxes. And we haven't even mentioned the punchlist for those who choose to bring children into the world: daycare, preschool, science projects, practice and games, driving lessons, financial aid forms, planning weddings, and the like.

The chief driver of to–do-ism is most likely worry about loss of identity: disquiet about diminishing personal value because the to-do list is growing shorter. If you're one of those folks who add an item to your to-do list *after* you've already done it so you can experience the spine-tingling rush of checking it off (okay, okay, I'm one of you), you need to pay attention here. (You probably just made a note in the margin, didn't you?) Some people respond to this sense of disappearing identity by creating a new kind of to-do list for the third age, by artificially pumping up their activities in an attempt to preserve their second age identities.

Without question, there's plenty to do during the second age. The to-do list is such an overwhelming factor during the second age that all of us face the risk that it will spill over into the third age with disproportionate force. To–do-ism can stunt, even block, a person's work in creating a new identity for the third age. And, forming a positive third age identity is the foundation for redefining retirement and sustaining growth during the third age.

RISK 5—SECOND AGE ADDICTIONS

Second age addictions form the other side of the coin to hanging on. Whereas people prone to hanging on continue to hold achievement as a prime motivating value of their actions in third age, second age addicts allow themselves to fall back passively into the behaviors that worked for them during the second age. If those driven to hang on labor to hold fast to the second age and its accoutrements, the addicts simply do not have the know-how, discipline, or gumption to replace the second age highs to which they have become accustomed. Second age addicts are unable to achieve the escape velocity needed to free themselves from second age gravity.

The primary driver of second age addiction is most likely an aversion to the risks involved in replacing a life infrastructure that is tried and true with a new infrastructure that is untested and uncertain. Yet, without a revitalized infrastructure to support third age goals and interests, it will be difficult to sustain second growth. We would try the metaphor of a lobster putting itself at mortal danger by shedding its current shell so that it can grow a larger shell. But the metaphor fails in that a lobster's new shell is not all that different in kind from the old: it's just bigger. Consider for the moment the notion of a lobster shedding its current shell so that it can take on a different kind of shell, for example a turtle shell, or a crab shell, because the lobster has *changed shape*. Form still must follow function. If you choose to use the six paradoxical principles to catalyze second growth in yourself, you will have transformed yourself in kind. You must leave behind your old shell.

But if you try to plan out each and every detail of your retirement in the manner that during your second age you planned a product launch, or prepped for a court case, or stepped through a medical diagnosis, or scrubbed budget numbers, you will treat third age as if it were an encore to second age. To get ready to change course, you will have to do a different kind of planning: a planning not inherently linear as during the second age, but a paradoxical kind of planning, planning that is imaginative and multidirectional, planning that requires reflection, creativity, and intense dialogue with loved ones and trusted friends.

We call it *third age planning*.

PLAN YOUR THIRD AGE AND RETIREMENT

GETTING READY TO CHANGE COURSE is crucial for a successful transition into third age and retirement. But how? What does solid preparation look like? Running the numbers is without question a vital part of the process: thorough financial planning is crucial. But many prospective retirees stop there. You know who you are: sneaking down to Human Resources to divine the most up-to-date gossip about an enhanced retirement package, cruising the Internet to get a leg up on how you can make your retirement nest egg (if you still have one) last as long as possible, working and reworking spreadsheets until your kitchen table looks like your tax guy's desk, and taking long weekends to reconnoiter prospective retirement communities. You can quote crime statistics like an FBI agent, rates of return like a banker, weather trends like a meteorologist, and entertainment options like a cruise director. If retirement planning were Three-Card Monty, you'd be a millionaire. So, how come you're still working? Consider Carol's predicament.

Carol works as an administrative supervisor for a services company that does third-party processing for clients around the world. The company's clients worship her for her responsiveness and can-do ethic. In her late fifties, she first put in her retirement paperwork five years ago and withdrew it after a plea from her boss that "the clients will go nuts if you leave." After taking a couple of years to train and coach a prospective replacement and introduce her to clients, Carol put in her retirement paperwork for a second time. Again, she withdrew the paperwork, this time because the sudden, severe illness of a grandchild forced her daughter to quit her job. (Her designated replacement in turn got discouraged and resigned, putting the company right back in the predicament from which it had just spent two years extracting itself.) Just before Carol was going, for the third time, to walk her paper down to Human Resources, the world changed, and she watched the value of her retirement fund shrink dramatically. The last time we talked with her, she commented, "I don't know anybody more ready, and less prepared, to retire than me. It's disheartening."

Not believing you have choices *is* disheartening. For Carol, the idea of beginning to create third age careers is an option for planning a fulfilling third age that she never considered. She's only just heard of it and is giving it thought. In discussions with our fifty-something friends who work in organizations, we have learned that many are eager to retire but have not yet done so because they are not sure precisely *what they will do* after they have retired. Logically, if the third age (like the second age) were still mainly about *doing*, then figuring out exactly what you will be doing after you have retired goes to the heart of the quandary: do I stay, or do I go?

Bill's twenty years of research, in particular his discovery of the six principles of growth and renewal, however, contradicts the common idea that the third age is predominantly about doing something new or doing something else. The third age is *not* only about *doing*, it is also about *becoming*. Both doing and becoming. The more Carol can learn about how to make that kind of transition and the more she comes to understand the six principles, the more effectively she will be able to plan for her own crossing over from the second age to the third age. Carol needs to do third age planning. And third age planning involves more than merely gathering data. Cindy's story illustrates one approach to getting ready to change course well before retirement appears on the radar screen.

Cindy: *I'm trying to reinvigorate the notion that one person can make a difference.*

After clerking for a federal judge and working at two firms, Cindy (fifty-three) got the opportunity to teach at a law school. From the beginning of her appointment, she had an avid interest in championing public interest matters and working in the arena of social responsibility, eventually teaching a course in poverty law. Connections with new friends encouraged her to expand her public interest work and gave her a taste of *social entrepreneurism.*

> I'm trying to reinvigorate the notion that one person can make a difference. It's a reawakening of a 1960s "Ah-hah" that everybody should care. There had been the civil rights movement, the antiwar movement, and the women's movement. They all seemed to disappear in the late 1970s. But I have learned that I can make a difference. Not only do I get to do good things myself, but also I get to nurture others in doing good. Every year I get to talk to twenty to forty law students and help them find ways to serve the public interest.

Cindy feels that she "dodged a bullet" when she decided to become a law professor because that move has given her opportunities to do "socially useful stuff." Having tested careers in television and law firms, she found that teaching law matched her core values and interests better than anything. Flexible boundaries allow her to move beyond organizational confines. She has a better chance of making a difference while making a living. Thriving as a social entrepreneur, she has been teaching a course in poverty law for almost ten years and has written articles on poverty and welfare. She has gotten involved in work for the homeless and has become more and more interested in public interest law. She helped create a public interest fellowship program at the law school. Law students identify a public interest need, develop a program to address that need, and write a proposal for a grant to fund the project. In addition to her involvement with the public interest fellowship program, Cindy mentors students with a passion about issues of social responsibility and has gotten involved with several ad hoc public interest projects, such as domestic violence.

My long-term goal is to change the culture of law schools with regard to issues of public interest, to teach lawyers to use their skills creatively for the public good. I want to spread the public interest fellowship program to other law schools. Public interest lawyers do not make a lot of money, and so we need to encourage young lawyers to get involved. A major magazine has expressed interest in doing a story on our public interest fellowship program. I'm excited about that.

A committed social entrepreneur, Cindy anticipates that retirement, still years down the road for her, will give her additional opportunity to pursue public interest causes. She intends to travel around the country, spreading the concept of the public interest fellowship program. At this point she is getting ready with third age planning. She has already begun to shape for herself a positive third age identity, although she is still rooted in the to-do's of the second age: preparing classes, coaching students, grading exams, and so on. When she determines that it is time to walk away, her transition to retirement will be made easier because she has already begun to redefine retirement as a time of opportunities. She knows that social entrepreneurism will form a key component in her third age careers. Her third age planning is well underway.

FIVE MAJOR TASKS FOR THIRD AGERS
APPROACHING RETIREMENT

WHEN IT COMES TO YOUR GETTING READY to change course, effective third age planning will not happen by accident. Neither are you apt to acquire the fresh perspectives you need by osmosis, or by divine intervention, or from tea leaves. Preparing yourself to navigate life after fifty requires disciplined focus to ensure that the major obstacles discussed above do not overwhelm you. Based on the five big risks for third agers approaching retirement, the authors—in conjunction with colleagues at The Center for Third Age Leadership—have developed a planning process for enabling people to accomplish five major tasks (in addition to sound financial planning) essential for redefining retirement and sustaining a fulfilling third age:

1. *Do Your Third Age Homework* (the antidote to being clueless): Get clued in. Found your third age decisions on information that is as accurate and up to date as you can.

2. *Change Negative Images of Aging* (the antidote to aging stereotypes): Accentuate the positive. Recognize and replace negative cultural stereotypes.

3. *Redefine Success From Achievement to Fulfillment* (the antidote to hanging on): Shift from worldly achievement to personal fulfillment. Heck yes, let's go.

4. *Build a New Identity on Paradox* (the antidote to to–do-ism): Stop being a do bee. Move from "either/or" to "both/and."

5. *Create a Third Age Infrastructure* (the antidote to second

age addictions): Try a new shell. Construct a supportive environment to sustain your second growth.

Let's not kid ourselves about how difficult it will be to achieve these five major tasks. The work is hard and practically out of the question to do alone—working with a third age coach or mentor is a pragmatic way to undertake the journey. Or work with a partner or trusted friend or colleague. The work of third age transformation will be ongoing; don't expect to be able to check off the accomplishment of these tasks on your to-do list anytime soon. You will find working through these tasks far different from most any task with which you were charged during the second age. Paradoxically, however, to get the process going you might discover that old tools from step-by-step action planning can be useful.

Task 1—Do Your Third Age Homework

Although third age planning is multidirectional and paradoxical in nature, doing your third age homework will require old-fashioned project planning: timelines, resources, and deadlines. Detailed financial planning? Absolutely: asset management, budgeting, and cashflow projections. Dueling daytimers? No question: neighborhood meetings, getaway trips, family celebrations, and community commitments. Consider, in addition, such questions as where you'd like to live during your third age. What factors are most vital to you in choosing a new community? What kind of home will best suit your emerging third age passions?

Vic's story in chapter 4 illustrates challenges related to relocating. Vic and his wife decided to pull up stakes to make a new home in what they would define as an ideal location. They did their homework. They explored the country and chose northern California because it fit so well with their expanding interests in spending more time outdoors for the whole year. This transition proved to be more challenging than they had thought it would be. They did more homework. Since their family was now scattered around the country, this location required more complicated arrangements for reconnecting. Time for more homework. But the benefits of the new community far outweighed the complications. Their homework had led them to the right place for their third age.

Ed's story in chapter 4 also demonstrates how doing your homework can help ensure that you avoid unrealistic expectations about the third age. In his early sixties Ed realized that he was nearing retirement and should start preparing for it. He attended a pre-retirement planning workshop at which he learned that he should think about *retiring to* rather than *retiring from*. That idea led him once again to revise his unfolding life. Without using the term, he began preparing for a graduation that would send him in a different but positive direction. When he finally graduated at sixty-five, he had a well-thought-out ten-year plan for an active lifestyle with defined areas and lots of flexibility. With his commencement underway, he said:

> I have a plan that will take me to when I'm seventy-five, when I will probably start winding down. For now I'm building a new business, spending more time with family and friends, traveling with my wife, staying active in sports and outdoor experiences, and community involvement. I like this life, especially the freedom. I don't have the pressure of "have to" anymore. I miss the university and friends there, but we stay in touch. I'm excited about what's coming next.

Ed thought long and hard about where he wanted his life to go. Some of his close friends had been retiring to the golf course or to Florida in their RVs. That lifestyle was not how he imagined leveraging his new freedom. He instead visualized the future as an opportunity to design an active life where he could devote himself to those activities and relationships that matter most to him. In planning his journey, Ed designed his life around key priorities. His life plan includes growing his beekeeping business, enjoying lots of free time with his wife, children, and first grandchild, traveling with his family, playing outdoors, and taking care of himself.

Task 2—Change Negative Images of Aging

Changing demeaning stereotypes of aging will first require you to recognize the array of negative images with which you have been imprinted. Take time to jot down both the positive and negative images that have been imprinted on you by the culture, by your social and religious beliefs, and by your experiences. Recall the books you've read, the songs you've listened to, and the movies and television shows you've seen. What were your parents like? Your grandparents? Your great aunts and uncles?

Initially, choose one negative image you'd like to let go off. Do not push away that image, but rather move yourself toward a positive image that you can use to replace the negative one. It's a common phenomenon that the more you try *not* to think of something, the more you *will* think of it. The harder you fight a negative image, the more it will hold you in its grip. Don't resist what you don't want; go toward what you do want. One by one you can walk away from belittling stereotypes of aging and walk toward positive images that can energize your third age transformation.

Susan's story in chapter 7 demonstrates how positive images of aging must displace the negative stereotypes with which most of us are imprinted. While recovering from cancer and a subsequent near-death experience from complications related to a ruptured appendix, Susan began pursing renewed spiritual development to bring what she called *the divine feminine* into her everyday life. Her enlarging sense of self has been influencing her entire life, including how she views and shapes her professional career. She has embraced learning, growth, and community building as key values in both her personal development and her choices of work. Keenly devoted to caring for her own wellbeing, keeping healthy has become a primary goal for Susan. In part, her self-care through her sixties aims to sustain her wellbeing, but it is also intended to retain strength and agility as she ages.

In her third age careers as an independent consultant, facilitator, coach, and social entrepreneur supporting women's leadership development, as well as community and environmental wellbeing, Susan has found or created numerous opportunities to express feminine principles. The scope of her work has broadened consistent with the increasing complexity of her vision. Working in both large organizations and small nonprofits, she strives to provide leadership consistent with her core values. In every aspect of her work, she endeavors to incorporate the feminine principles of creativity, communion, and collaboration. As her life circles around a core of commitments and possibilities and expands in new directions, she experiences continued transformation. Because she abhors the cultural degradation of older people, and in particular the degradation of older women, she wants to affirm her own worth and the value of older women everywhere as she pursues her vision, continues her work, and sustains her growth.

For over ten years Susan has been building a robust third age life portfolio, and her ensemble continues to expand.

TASK 3—REDEFINE SUCCESS FROM ACHIEVEMENT TO FULFILLMENT

The first age (school) centers on preparation, the second age (jobs) focuses on achievement, the third age strives for fulfillment, and the fourth age attains completion. Another way of saying this is learning, doing, becoming, and integration, although learning, doing, becoming, and integration do not follow each other in a purely sequential fashion. We want a mix of learning, doing, becoming, and integration in all four ages in the life course, but what we spend most of our time on does shift from one age to the next.

Most of us have a grasp of what learning and doing are— been there, done that—but for many of us *becoming* is more elusive (as is *integration*). Take a moment to recall a time in your life when time stood still for you, a time when you had no sense of time, a time when you felt you were experiencing everything you are in one moment. Csikszentmihalyi's *flow*. While it's obvious we want learning, doing, and becoming to be part of all our ages (just like it's obvious we want positive images of aging), it's hard to overcome a lifetime of cultural conditioning. To shake up this conditioning, ask yourself, "What legacy do I want to leave? How do I want to be remembered by those who matter most to me?" What matters most to you? What do you want to feel: peaceful, challenged, needed, free? What activities, or lack of activities, will create and sustain these feelings for you?

Vic's story provides a model for redefining success from achievement in the second age to fulfillment in the third age.

Moving from one to the other was not a step down for him; it was a graduation. The quality of your retirement will depend on how you choose to perceive it. If you see your journey after retirement as a descent after a career peak, as a diminishment, you're likely to experience decline in various aspects of your life. If you let it, your retirement can become a gradual hibernation. Vic and his wife, however, reframed their retirement as a graduation, a grand entrance, an esplanade to new *life peaks*.

For many people retirement signifies an ending rather than a beginning, but retirement can offer an opportunity to address new challenges that lead to advances in personal growth. Vic knew that he and his wife of nearly forty years had much more life to live, and they did not want to spend it the prescriptive ways pre-retirement programs typically suggest. He began a journey of self-discovery and self-redefinition. His graduation gave him the chance to realize a dream by tapping dormant potential and helping others advance. Commencement opened a side of his personality that had been suppressed in a thirty-year career with a major corporation. By redefining retirement, he has been changing course to create a rich and fulfilling third age.

TASK 4—BUILD A NEW IDENTITY ON PARADOX

An *either/or* worldview is imprinted on most of us in the western world. If something is black, it *cannot* be white. And we Westerners have grown adept at defending our either/or outlook by explaining deviations as exceptions: "That's the exception that proves the rule." But the world is not an either/or cosmos, but rather it is a *both/and* universe. Is light a wave or a particle? Remember that debate. Turns out the answer is, yes. The comedian Steven Wright asks, "If the universe is all there is, and it's expanding, what's it expanding into?" Hmmm. What's the old saying? There are two kinds of people in the world: people who think there are two kinds of people in the world, and people who don't. Either/or limits possibilities.

Black and white thinking is associated with immaturity; seeing shades of gray bespeaks maturity and wisdom. To create a new third age identity, you will have to abandon an either/or view and accept a both/and way of looking at things: yin and yang, light and dark, spirit and flesh. Paradoxes. You will have to make a wish to take you beyond the mundane options your conditioning has taught you to settle for. Go for it, but do so in a way that you can recognize your wish when you get it. Then, ask "why" the wish is important to you. Ask why again, and again. Ask yourself, "What do I want" and "Why don't I already have it?" Finally, ask, "In what ways might I have both?" You've created a personal paradox.

Eva's story in chapter 5 illustrates the power of building a third age identity based on paradox. Eva could have easily succumbed to the chronic pain cause by her fall. Instead of pushing back against the pain during her convalescence, she used the time to explore hidden dimensions in herself and to discover her potential for new experiences. The accident also gave her a much-needed message—slow down. Reflection sparked creativity that had been lying fallow deep within her. Recalling aspects of herself she had forgotten, she began to record her memories and explore a past that she had set aside. She created a different sense of herself, one that she believes is more appropriate for her third age.

The changes she was making in her life as a result of the fall and her prolonged recovery led her to a new insight. In retrospect, she saw that her accident had provided an entrance into a new way of living. Eva had a firm sense that she was experiencing "a big spurt of creativity. She believes that most people over fifty need an outside force to wake them up: an event to knock them off course, to provoke discovery of the richness within them and the possibilities in front of them. Applying her creativity to her own life, she is finding a way that is qualitatively and quantitatively different from anything she had previously known or even imagined. The manner in which she responded to the fall fired her personal transformation. Eva has discovered in her life a totally unexpected outcome never dreamed of when she first took retirement.

TASK 5—CREATE A THIRD AGE INFRASTRUCTURE

Mike's story in chapter 5 points up the criticality of infrastructure to sustaining second growth during the third age. While barreling ahead on his mission "to find inner peace in a damn big hurry," Mike met Andrew and realized that he had found a mentor and a role model. Andrew was living the kind of life that Mike felt would provide him inner peace. Although working with a third age coach or mentor might not in the narrow sense be viewed as *infrastructure*, a coach or a mentor can play a vital role in helping build the environment needed to sustain second growth after fifty. So can a spouse. The relationship Mike has with his second wife provides a supportive infrastructure for his growth. When Mike decided to get back into art, he opened a gallery. His original intent was to use the gallery to display his own paintings, but local artists came in and asked him to show their works as well. After six months, so many local artists had asked to have their work displayed that he had to expand the gallery. The gallery has not been all that rewarding in financial terms, but it has enabled him to make many new friends in his community. Mike's gallery is also infrastructure.

Mike enlarged his third age careers by starting a consultancy in master planned communities, with a special interest in designing communities for Baby Boomers. Although Mike continues to spend most of his time and energy on painting and on the gallery, he enjoys consulting because he is doing it with people whom he likes and respects. Many of his current friends started off as clients of the consulting practice. Mike's consultancy is additional infrastructure. With a lifestyle filled with creative stuff and people he loves, he looks forward to shaping emerging third age careers where success will be measured in terms of his social contribution. Spiritual growth is still a priority for Mike, and he continues to read a lot. He wants to mature in his painting and works hard to make his gallery successful. And he will continue consulting on master planned communities. Mike's relationship with his mentor, his wife, the art gallery, and the consultancy provide him the infrastructure crucial to sustaining his growth, his learning, his painting, and his work, four of his key third age passions.

This book abounds with other examples of third agers shedding their lobster shells so that they can inhabit a new environment. Betty (chapter 4) revived her decorating skills to make her home more beautiful and welcoming. She cultivated a garden that fills her home with flowers, and she invites friends and neighbors over to enjoy her home, the flowers, and each other. El (chapter 4) and his wife moved to a farm in northwestern Maine, where she opened an antique store and he set up a studio where he could do woodcarving. Rebecca (chapter 5) and her husband have invested energy, creativity, and love into a carefully designed space that expresses who they are and what they care about. Her paintings and photos cover the walls of every room, hallway, and stairwell, while tables and shelves hold her sculptures and ceramics. Carl (chapter 6) enrolled in a clinical pastoral education program to pursue his aspirations to become a hospital chaplain and has recently accepted a leadership position in the Presbyterian Church. Susan (chapter 7) concluded that her new self would be better situated in a village close to water and a forest. Following this vision, she moved out of a major metropolitan area and into a new home in a river village, where she lives within a housing cluster.

SEVENTEEN LESSONS FROM THIRD AGERS (REVISITED)

WE ALL HAVE MUCH TO LEARN from the third agers who have graciously shared their remarkable stories. As a tribute to them, but also to provide you with a reminder of the hard but joyful work that lies ahead, we will restate the seventeen lessons from chapters 4 through 7, in addition to the five major tasks just discussed.

Start with Yourself: As you look ahead to the next leg in your life's journey, it's time to turn inward before changing course. You possess talents and interests that are waiting to be discovered. What are they? It's time to explore within. Dream a little—dream a lot! Put yourself in a different context within which you're freer to let new thoughts enter. Play with them. Share your dreams with your spouse or partner, a close friend, or a mentor or coach. Check inward, check outward.

Dig Deep: Making a transition from the second age into a redefined third age requires thorough self-examination. Digging deep will require a combination of shameless self-honesty, ongoing patience with yourself, and disciplined exploration of aspects of yourself that you may have been avoiding. Taking an intense look inside demands imagination, commitment, courage, and tenacity. Find the passion that makes your soul sing. Hold up a mirror, and stare into it long and hard. Don't blink.

Consider a Guide: Digging deep is hard work, and being willing to accept what you find hidden way down there might be disturbing. Underestimating the difficulty of prolonged self-examination would be foolhardy. If you think you will need help when you hold up the mirror to yourself, get it—someone to mentor, guide, and inspire you on your journey to a redefined retirement. Recall Dante's disclosure in *Paradiso*, "Dazed by bewilderment, to my guide I turned." He asked for directions.

One, Two, Three—Let Go: As you review all the good things and achievements that have been integral to your second age, be prepared to let go. It's scary to leave a place where you're known, recognized, and appreciated—like leaving home all over again. Review where you've been and what you've got now, and shift to where you're going and what you dream of becoming? How are your personal attachments—your pianos—preventing you from going for it? Lighten your load.

Figure Out What Success Looks Like *for You*: As you see your commencement into the third age taking you in new directions, you'll need to develop for yourself new measures of success. Success within the process of building a third age life portfolio lies in the quality of your unfolding life. What do you want not *from* life, but rather *for* life? Turn off the noise inside your own head, and listen to the music your soul is making. The music will be the measure of your success. Listen to it.

Give IT a Name That Inspires You, That Guides You: Life after fifty is not going to be like the life you've had. For *your* retirement, choose a name that will free you to reframe *it* in a personal, inspirational way. Graduation!? Protirement!? Refirement!? Make up your own. What matters is that you design your new life around core values, interests, and passions, both yours and those of the person, or people, with whom you intend to share your third age. What's in a name? A lot.

Refashion Your Identity: Refashioning your identity is the cornerstone as you build new meaning for your third age and retirement. You will redefine the person you can become by building a third age life portfolio. Reshaping your identity will require that you reposition, retune, or replace many instruments in your orchestra. You've got work to do, and play to do, and connecting and re-connecting to do, and healing to do, and creating to do. Get going.

Get Started on Your Portfolio and Keep on Painting: Your life portfolio will be the practical way for you to define an evolving personal identity during your third age. Now is the time to attend to your several loves. The secret in putting together a third age life portfolio that sustains your growth is to practice creative balancing of multiple interests and commitments. This balancing act involves embracing paradoxes at every turn along the way.

Let Your Flow Be Like an Eagle's Wing: Diversification in your life portfolio is crucial for long-term success. The self you want to become is not a biomechanical biped in motion, but a historical process in which you become your own story. Your challenge is to organize your interests into a diversified portfolio aimed at yielding the story you want to become. Create a story your grandchildren and grand nieces and nephews will want to tell their grandchildren and grand nieces and nephews.

Free Yourself for What's Important: Typically, retirement gives people a great increase in personal freedom. This gift of freedom confounds many retirees, driving them by default to activity for activity's sake. Avoid the danger of seeing your third age primarily as freedom from the many things you're tired of doing. You must frame in a meaningful way the increase in freedom you experience as earlier necessities diminish. Take off the shackles inside your head.

Do Work That MATTERS: No matter how you regard the day jobs you've had during second age, work can express who you want to become after fifty. Your new work will also be one way for you to experience flow, a passage to your new identity; and it will become part of your legacy. Take advantage of the opportunities provided by the third age. Determining the criteria for what *matters* is a profoundly personal choice and must flow from your vision for yourself for your third age. What matters to you?

Find New Ways to Work: Work is a way to nurture and express a fuller sense of self and sometimes a deepening spirituality. During the second age you doubtless heard maxims such as, "Work smarter, not harder." In the third age, work paradoxically, work imaginatively, and work metaphysically: work *into* yourself. Shape your third age careers in response to what you feel you've been called to do after your second age careers concluded. Reinvent your work, and yourself.

Create the Right Space: If you think of the shaping of your life story as a drama, then you'll know that your drama has to be staged against the backdrop of the right kind of set. Choose for yourself a space and surroundings that fit the self you are trying to become. Or redesign your current space and surroundings. You don't necessarily have to move, but it's essential to invest yourself in designing your personal space to fit the portfolio life you are creating. Chuck that old shell.

Expect—and Accept—the Unexpected: The third age will surprise you with both joyful news and sorrowful news. Learn to embrace these surprises and to transform them into springboards for propelling second growth. Find ways to use the unexpected as pathways to greater self-understanding, as fuel for self-growth, as a reminder of the fragility of cherished relationships, and as a way to move closer to the reality you most truly desire. Welcome surprises.

Build Connections to People of All Ages: Successful third agers not only have wisdom to share, but they also learn from people of all ages and backgrounds. Build relationships with a diversity of people, not only with people of your own age, gender, race, or profession. Fly with as many different kinds of birds as you can. Appreciate, value, and cultivate boundarylessness. Boundaryless learning. Boundaryless relationships. Boundaryless creativity.

Be Greek: Stay Balanced: Weave together a rich, brightly colored, intricate self-tapestry. Your emerging self-awareness in creative balancing will point you in a unifying direction, to an experience of personal integration that is the core of integrity, to oneness with the universe. Whatever you're comfortable with calling it—the golden mean, a balanced lifestyle, holism, or the omega point—recognize that finding a way to live harmoniously is crucial to prospering in your third age. Conduct your own orchestra. Give every section a chance to be heard.

Live Vitally: Our culture floods us with disheartening, stereotypical images of life after fifty. Just say no to this hooey. Create your portfolio life with engagement, enthusiasm, and élan. Learn from our storytellers: make sure that you keep your spirit soaring by keeping your body and mind strong and vital. Take on new challenges. Go boldly where you have not gone before. As with our storytellers, also for you, Rabbi Ben Ezra's words will ring true, "The best is yet to be!" Go for IT!

"THE BEST IS YET TO BE"

RETIREMENT POSES SOME OF THE MOST CHALLENGING questions we have ever faced. Who am I and what kind of person do I want to become? Where do I want my life to go next? What legacy will I leave? The concept of retirement needs new meaning if we are to prevent a colossal waste of human potential. One by one the trailblazers in this book have been intrepidly addressing the challenges of retirement *by redefining it*. Most don't even think of themselves as retired. They have been able to free themselves of misconceptions and stereotypes that limit creative thinking about how to navigate life after fifty.

Rather than seeing retirement as a period of idleness, more are seeing it as a period of opportunity—not a snug safe harbor but a bold change of course on a bold new voyage. This opportunity includes freedom to spend more time with family, to invest in leisure activities and learning, to travel, to make a difference in the community, and to build third age careers. Virtually all of the people we've interviewed, who might be considered to have retired, say that retirement does not apply to their unfolding lives. They are not anchored, but underway. They're advancing, not retiring. Full speed ahead.

People in their fifties, sixties, and seventies have been creatively designing, or redesigning, their lives and exhibiting new, mature growth just when a person might—as conditioned by stereotypes of aging—expect decline. Like pioneers on a new frontier, they have been opening up a thirty-year life bonus in the second half of life, making it the best period in their lives. They are building new identities with third age life portfolios. Their stories tell each of us in quite persuasive terms: *My third age can be the best time in my life.* It is an opportunity for optimal development. The twenty-first century gives us a first-time-in-human-history opportunity.

The design you bring to your individual third age will call for redefining your retirement as mindfully as you have prepared for your second age career. Reflect on, dream about, and plan for how you might wish to change the course of your life. By doing so, you'll be prepared to redesign your retirement all over again when you enter your fourth age, the period of completion. Robert Browning's Rabbi Ben Ezra tenders, "The best is yet to be. The last of life for which the first way made." Do you believe it? Or do you see yourself as over the hill? Can you see yourself climbing to new heights? Will you mark your third age with **D** words such as *decline, degeneration, deterioration,* and *disengagement,* or with **R** words like *renewal, redesign, reinvention, rediscovery,* and *redirection*? How are you going to change course?

The take-away of the storytellers in this book is electrifying possibility: second growth represents a new option in your life course. Here's the new course: self-discovery, invention, and the redesign of your life to create the person you've always wanted to become. Beware, for there are paradoxes to take with you. To go forward in realizing a renewed self, you will need to go back and recover the young self you left behind.

To take control of your life course in the face of great uncertainty you will have to learn to let go and allow the creative process to germinate. Give yourself permission to unpack elements for which you had neither appreciation nor time in your second age. The second harvest in your life will reap the output of creativity that may not have been ready to be tapped in the first half of life. It's time for you to start imagining your life with a thirty-year bonus and what you might become after fifty. As you change course, you too will discover that the best *is* yet to be. But only if you believe it, and make it so.

Notes

INTRODUCTION

xiv An International Conference *From Ageing to Ageing Well* was held in Montreal, Quebec, October 3–5, 2004, with participants from twenty-five countries. Bill Sadler gave a key presentation, "Redefining Retirement with Life Portfolios and Third Age Careers," sharing the platform with Robert Kahn, co-author of *Successful Aging*, and George Vaillant, author of *Aging Well*.

xv William A. Sadler, *The Third Age: Six Principles of Growth and Renewal After Forty* (Cambridge, MA: Perseus, 2000, 2001). It has been translated into German, Dutch, and Korean.

xvi The Center for Third Age Leadership, LLC was founded in 2002 to apply the six principles to the workforce. It offers workshops, retreats, seminars, consulting, and coaching, with a focus on life renewal and pre-retirement planning. Visit www.thirdagecenter.com.

CHAPTER 1

5 Erik H. Erikson, Joan M. Erikson, and Helen Q. Kivnick, *Vital Involvement in Old Age* (New York: W. W. Norton, 1986), 297.

5 "Reinventing Retirement," AARP *Bulletin*, December 2002.

6 Martha McNeil Hamilton, "Embarking in a Second Act: More Older Workers Are Skipping Retirement to Try New Careers," *Washington Post*, April 19, 2003, D-12.

7 Using Internal Revenue Service life-expectancy tables and 2000 census data, as of 2007 the Baby Boom generation will collectively live another 2.7 billion years, close to a trillion

days. A UN conference on aging predicts that by 2150 one-third of the world's population will be over sixty, *San Francisco Chronicle*, April 23, 2002, A-17.

8   See Helen Dennis's comments in the above AARP article. See also Helen Dennis, "The New Retirement," in *Working Through Demographic Change*, William K. Zinke and Susan Tattershall, eds. (Boulder, CO: Human Resources Center, 2000).

CHAPTER 2

18   One of the best books to explode negative stereotypes of aging was by the husband and wife team K. Warner Schaie and Sherry L. Willis, *Adult Development and Aging*, second edition (Boston: Little, Brown, and Company, 1986).

19   In 2003 an Internet poll received thousands of responses, many from people over sixty.

20   Paul B. Baltes and Margret M. Baltes, eds., *Successful Aging: Perspectives From The Behavioral Sciences* (Cambridge: Cambridge University Press, 1990).

20   John W. Rowe and Robert L. Kahn, *Successful Aging* (New York: Pantheon, 1998).

20   Thomas T. Perls, Margery H. Silver, and John F. Lauerman, *Living to 100: Lessons in Living to Your Maximum Potential at Any Age* (New York: Basic Books, 2000).

21   Oliver Sacks, "A Neurologist's Notebook: The Mind's Eye," *The New Yorker*, July 28, 2003, 48–59.

22   In addition to United States census data available on the Internet, see Judith Treas, "Older Americans in the 1990s and Beyond," *Population Bulletin* (Washington, DC), Vol. 50, No. 2, May, 1995. For more information see www.prb.org.

23   Walter M. Bortz II, *Dare to Be 100: 99 Steps to a Long, Healthy Life* (New York: Simon and Schuster, 1996).

27   Robert Browning, "Rabbi Ben Ezra," *Selected Poetry* (New York: Modern Library, 1951).

CHAPTER 3

35   Ellen J. Langer, *Mindfulness* (Reading, MA: Addison Wesley, 1989).

43   Becca Levy, Martin Slade, Suzanne Kunkel, and Stanislav Kasl, "Longevity Increased by Positive Self-Perceptions of Aging," *Journal of Personality and Social Psychology*, 2002, Vol. 83 No. 2, 261–270.

45   Mitch Albom, *Tuesdays with Morrie: An Old Man, a Young Man, and Life's Greatest Lesson* (New York: Doubleday, 1997), 156.

48   Explanation provided by David A. Garvin, *Learning in Action: A Guide to Putting the Learning Organization to Work* (Boston: Harvard Business School Press, 2000).

48   Rosamund S. Zander and Benjamin Zander, *The Art of Possibility: Transforming Professional and Personal Life* (Boston: Harvard Business School Press, 2000), 56–63.

48   Mihaly Csikszentmihalyi, *Flow: The Psychology of Optimal Experience* (New York: Harper and Row, 1990).

50   Ashley Montagu, *Growing Young*, second edition (Granby, MA: Bergin and Garvey, 1988).

51   Jerome S. Bruner, *In Search of Mind* (New York: Harper and Row, 1983).

54   Michael Gurian, *What Could He Be Thinking?: How a Man's Mind Really Works* (New York: St. Martin's, 2003).

54   Allan Chinen, *Beyond the Hero* (New York: Jeremy Tarcher, 1993).

59   Charles Handy, *The Age of Unreason* (Boston: Harvard Business School Press, 1990), 177. For over fifteen years this British business writer has been pointing out the challenges, opportunities, and probable consequences of greater longevity and a revitalized third age for individuals, organizations, and society.

61   See Jimmy Carter's self-portrait in *The Virtues of Aging* (New York: Ballantine, 1998). For a complementary perspective on maturation as a virtuous enterprise, see the insightful application of Aristotle's philosophy in a contemporary attempt to build a balanced, rewarding, purposeful life by James O'Toole, *Creating*

the *Good Life: Applying Aristotle's Wisdom to Find Meaning and Happiness* (New York: Rodale, 2004).

63 George E. Vaillant, *Aging Well: Surprising Guideposts to a Happier Life from the Landmark Harvard Study of Adult Development* (Boston: Little, Brown, 2002).

65 Maya Angelou's comments were given during an interview with Oprah Winfrey.

66 Thomas Berry, *Befriending the Earth: A Theology of Reconciliation between Humans and the Earth* (Mystic, CT: Twenty-Third Publications, 1991), 132. See also his *The Great Work: Our Way into the Future* (New York: Bell Tower, 1999).

67 See Rowe and Kahn's *Successful Aging* for advice on taking care of your health. Edward Schneider, also a member of the *MacArthur Study of Successful Aging*, has written a lucid, practical book about promoting optimal health. See Edward L. Schneider and Elizabeth Miles, *Ageless: Take Control of Your Age and Stay Youthful for Life* (New York: Rodale, 2003).

68 Robert M. Freedman and David N. Grant, *The Secret Sayings of Jesus – According to the Gospel of Thomas* (London: Fontana, 1960). This rendition was taken from Charles Handy's *The Hungry Spirit* (New York: Broadway, 1998), 103. Elaine Pagels presents a similar translation of this text in her *Beyond Belief: The Secret Gospel of Thomas* (New York: Random House, 2003).

CHAPTER 4

95   Henry David Thoreau, *Walden; or, Life in the Woods* (New York: Holt, Rinehart and Winston, 1965).

103 A similar approach to developing your creative potential has been provided by Peter M. Senge in *The Fifth Discipline* (New York: Doubleday, 1990). See his discussion of personal mastery.

105 Stephen King, *Misery* (New York: Signet/Penguin Putnam, 1987).

CHAPTER 5

109 Horace Walpole coined the word *serendipity* in 1774. The late Robert K. Merton has written about serendipities in sociology and the history of science: *The Travels and Adventures of Serendipity: A Study in Sociological Semantics and the Sociology of Science* (Princeton: Princeton University Press, 2003).

110 John A. Clausen, *American Lives: Looking Back at the Children of the Great Depression* (New York: The Free Press, 1993), 236–240.

111 George Vaillant, *Aging Well*, 32, 131, 223, 243.

112 The psychiatrist Gene D. Cohen has also emphasized the potential of human creativity in the aging process. See *The Creative Age: Awakening Human Potential in the Second Half of Life* (New York: Quill/Avon, Harper Collins, 2000). His book is filled with anecdotes of people who have tapped creative reservoirs in their later years.

112 Mihaly Csikszentmihalyi, *Creativity: Flow and the Psychology of Discovery and Invention* (New York: Harper Collins, 1996).

129 Peter F. Drucker, "The New Pluralism," in *Leading Beyond the Walls*, Frances Hesselbein, Marshall Goldsmith, and Iain Somerville, eds. (San Francisco: Jossey-Bass, 1999).

145 Dante Alighieri, "Canto XXII," *Divina Commedia di Dante: Paradiso* (Project Gutenberg E-Text #999: http://sailor.gutenberg.org/etext97/3ddcd09.txt, 1997).

146 Robert Ornstein, *Multimind: A New Way of Looking at Human Behavior* (New York: Doubleday Anchor Books, 1989).

CHAPTER 6

150 Representative Pepper quoted in Gene Cohen, *The Creative Age*, 66.

153 Barry Curnow and John McLean Fox, *Third Age Careers: Meeting the Corporate Challenge* (Hampshire, England: Gower, 1994). These

258   Changing Course

two British consultants reported on companies that were trying out third age careers in the 1990s. We have developed our own concept of third age careers, based on our research in the United States. More recent, in 70: *The New 50: Retirement Management: Retaining the Energy and Expertise of Experienced Employees* (Pittsburgh: DDI Press, 2007), William C. Byham develops a similar idea, which he calls retirement management. It's a new approach in human resources for organizations that want to retain the wisdom and expertise of senior employees, rather than lose them through retirement.

158 Stephen M. Dent and James H. Krefft, *Powerhouse Partners: A Blueprint for Building Organizational Culture for Breakaway Results* (Palo Alto, CA: Davies-Black, 2004).

186 Pierre Teilhard de Chardin, *Christianity and Evolution* (New York: Harcourt Brace and Jovanovich, 1969).

CHAPTER 7

189 *San Francisco Chronicle*, June 14, 2004, A-4.

191 Linda Clever has developed an organization that promotes renewal among healthcare professionals. See www.renewnow. org/RenewOmeter.

191 Mihaly Csikszentmihalyi, *Good Business* (New York: Viking, 2003), 169.

217 Sebastian De Grazia claimed that the Greeks invented *leisure*. Different from free time, it represents freedom to devote oneself to activities that are ends in themselves. See *Of Time, Work, and Leisure* (New York: Doubleday Anchor, 1964). For insights into Greek culture see C. M. Bowra, *The Greek Experience* (New York: New American Library, 1957).

CHAPTER 8

232 David Bornstein, *How to Change the World: Social Entrepreneurs and*

the *Power of New Ideas* (New York: Oxford University Press, 2004). In *Prime Time: How Baby Boomers Will Revolutionize Retirement and Transform America* (New York: Public Affairs, 2000), Marc Freedman recommends that third agers redefine work after retirement by engaging in socially significant volunteer enterprises. His organization, Civic Ventures, has been promoting creative volunteer initiatives that specifically benefit society.

Cover design: Aimee Carlos, Wildflower Graphics,
wildflowergraphics@earthlink.net

Book design: Dianne Nelson, Shadow Canyon Graphics,
shadowcanyongraphics.com, dnshadow@earthlink.net

INDEX

midlife crisis. *See* middle age
Mike's story, 137–143, 242–243
Miles, Elizabeth, 256
mindful reflection vs. risk taking.
    See six principles of growth and
    renewal
mindfulness, 35, 39
Mindfulness, 255
Misery, 105, 256
Monhegan Island, 205
Montagu, Ashley, 50, 255
Mr. Spock, 25
Multimind, 146, 257
Murdoch, Rupert, 149
music. *See* the arts
Mystic River, 151

National Executive Service Corps,
    173
Native Americans. *See* American
    Indians
negative self-image, 43
neotony, 50
Newman Center, 194

Of Time, Work, and Leisure, 258
O'Keefe, Georgia, 150
old scripts, 33–35, 39–40. *See also*
    aging stereotypes
omega point, 186–187, 249. *See also*
    spirituality
optimal development and growth,
    xvi, 20–22, 48–49, 57–58. *See also*
    human development
optimism. *See* realistic optimism
Ornstein, Robert, 146, 257
O'Toole, James, 255
outdoor activities, 78, 84, 93–94,
    98–99, 121–124, 135–136, 163,
    199, 205, 211–212. *See also*
    exercise

Outward Bound, 122–123,
    125–126, 128–130, 144, 146,
    158, 204–205, 216

paganism, 196
Pagels, Elaine, 256
Paige, Satchel, 50, 151
Paradiso, 145, 245
paradoxes. *See* six principles of
    growth and renewal
patriarchy, 54, 77, 196. *See also*
    masculinity
Peace Corps, 58
Pepper, Claude, 150
Perls, Thomas, 254
perpetual sabbatical. *See*
    sabbatical
personal freedom, 37, 215–216,
    247
personal freedom vs. intimacy. *See*
    six principles of growth and
    renewal
Picasso, 150
planning. *See* third age planning
poetry. *See* the arts
Ponce de Leon, 226
positive third age identity. *See* six
    principles of growth and
    renewal
post-career career, 159, 162, 165,
    184. *See also* third age careers
post-institutional identity, 9,
    42–43
Powerhouse Partners, vi, 258
pre-retirement planning. *See*
    retirement planning
Prime Time, 259
principles of growth and renewal.
    See six principles of growth and
    renewal
protirement, 8, 193, 216, 246
psychodrama, 113, 119–120, 145

How to order *Changing Course*

To order *Changing Course* online using a major credit card through PayPal, go to www.ChangingCourseBook.com. All credit card orders must be processed online.

To order by mail for delivery to U.S. postal addresses, mail in this form with a check or money order in U.S. dollars. Make check or money order out to "The Center for Third Age Leadership, LLC." Full remittance must be included with all mail orders.

CHANGING COURSE ORDER FORM

Name _____ Phone _____

E-Mail (optional) _____

Address _____

_____

City _____ State _____ ZIP _____

*For United States Postal Addresses Only

	Copies	Amount	Item Total
Changing Course		$18.95	
S&H per copy (2008)		$4.95	
Sales tax per copy for Colorado residents only		$1.64	
Grand Total			

*For international and bulk orders, send queries to *orders@ChangingCourseBook.com*

Mail completed form along with full remittance to:
The Center for Third Age Leadership Press
3414 East Jamison Place
Centennial, CO 80122-3523

How to order *Changing Course*

To order *Changing Course* online using a major credit card through PayPal, go to www.ChangingCourseBook.com. All credit card orders must be processed online.

　　To order by mail for delivery to U.S. postal addresses, mail in this form with a check or money order in U.S. dollars. Make check or money order out to "The Center for Third Age Leadership, LLC." Full remittance must be included with all mail orders.

CHANGING COURSE ORDER FORM

Name _____ Phone _____

E-Mail (optional) _____

Address _____

_____

City _____ State _____ ZIP _____

*For United States Postal Addresses Only

	Copies	Amount	Item Total
Changing Course		$18.95	
S&H per copy (2008)		$4.95	
Sales tax per copy for Colorado residents only		$1.64	
Grand Total			

*For international and bulk orders, send queries to *orders@ChangingCourseBook.com*

Mail completed form along with full remittance to:
The Center for Third Age Leadership Press
3414 East Jamison Place
Centennial, CO 80122-3523